Paper Mache

DRAGONS

**Making Dragons
& Trophies
using
Paper &
Cloth Mache**

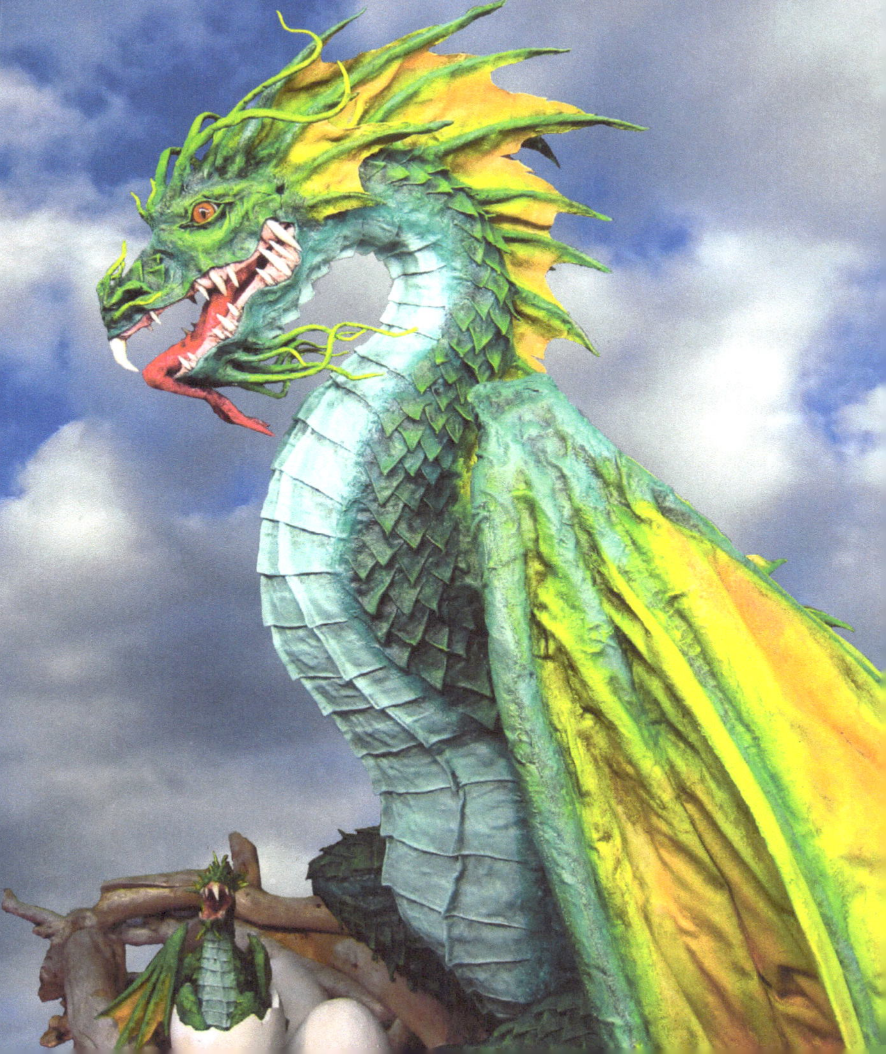

Dan Reeder

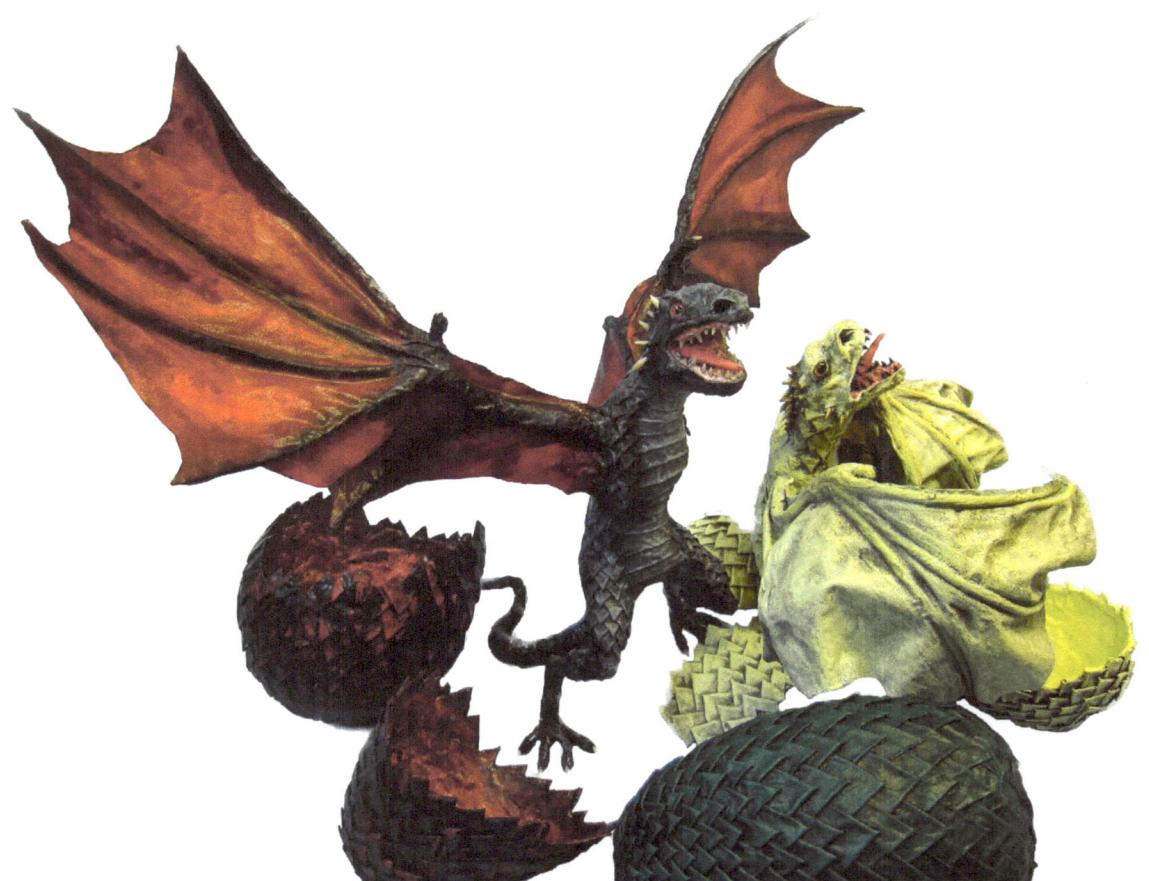

Contents

Introduction

I love dragons. I'm in good company. Dragons appear in the lore of virtually every culture and region of the world. There is something wonderful about big, flying, reptilian beasts that toast and eat their prey on the spot. With the advent of the TV series "Game of Thrones" and the movie "How to Train Your Dragon 6" (it's coming), interest in dragons in the United States couldn't be higher. It's probably good that they don't really exist. We'd all have them as pets. They would be selling live goats at Petco as dragon food. I'd be the first on my block to own one. But alas (sniff), they don't exist. Still, that hasn't stopped me from filling my house with dragons. In fact, I consider myself incredibly fortunate. I know how to make them. After watching Daenerys Targaryen emerge from the bonfire with little dragons clinging to her, I thought, "I want a little Drogon!" And I made him. How great is that?

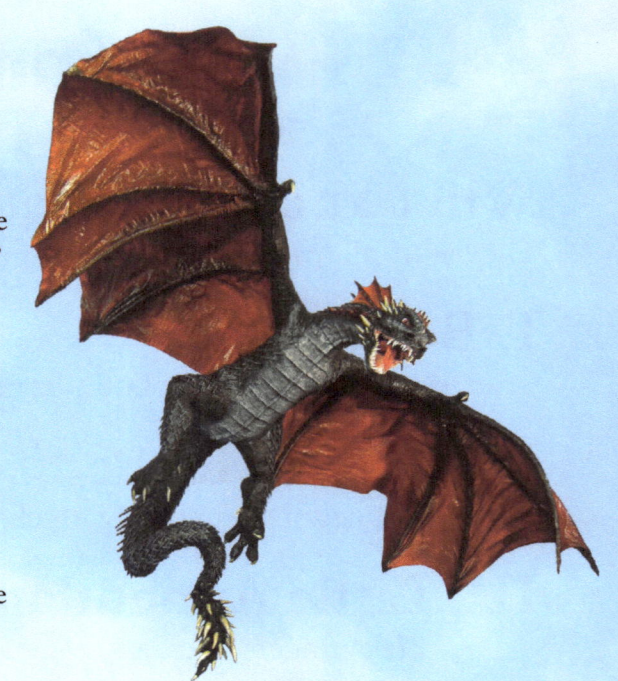

I'm going to show you how I make my dragons in this book. I've added a section about dragon trophies for those of you who just want a nice dragon head above the mantel. But first, a little about "paper mache." The French coined the phrase, "papier mâché," which literally meant chewed or mashed paper. They squished the stuff into "French Art." This version of paper mache persists today. There are artists who use a mashed paper recipe, usually made with toilet paper (or newspaper), mixed with glue. There are several commercial products that are essentially pulverized paper. Add water and sculpt. These "paper clay" methods are touted as easier, "less messy" versions of traditional paper mache. I've used them all and found them to be unwieldy (you are sculpting with putty) and very unforgiving when dry. And they just don't allow for the kind of detail you want in a dragon. Oh...and they **are** messy.

Don't get me wrong. I'm not against messy art. Art should be messy! The way I do paper mache certainly is. Gloriously so. I use a variation of what has been described as "traditional" paper mache even though there is nothing French or mashed about it (which is why I finally gave up using the French spelling and symbols). It involves covering something with newspaper strips using flour and water paste. No one really knows how this began, but if you are of a certain age (that is, if you are old) you probably made a piggy by covering a balloon with paper mache (and adding toilet paper tube legs). It was fun, but a very low level art project. Some artists apply this kind of paper mache over a substructure of wood and chicken wire. That is, they sculpt with chicken wire and then add a few layers of paper mache. In contrast, I sculpt with pieces of paper mache balls that I put together with masking tape. I then add a "skin" of cloth dipped in white glue. This adds considerable strength and allows for details that you just can't get with paper alone (or paper clay). It's perfect for dragon wings, as you will discover. I invented this process and dubbed it "cloth mache" in my first book, The Simple Screamer: A Guide to the Art of Papier and Cloth Mâché (1984, Gibbs Smith Publisher).

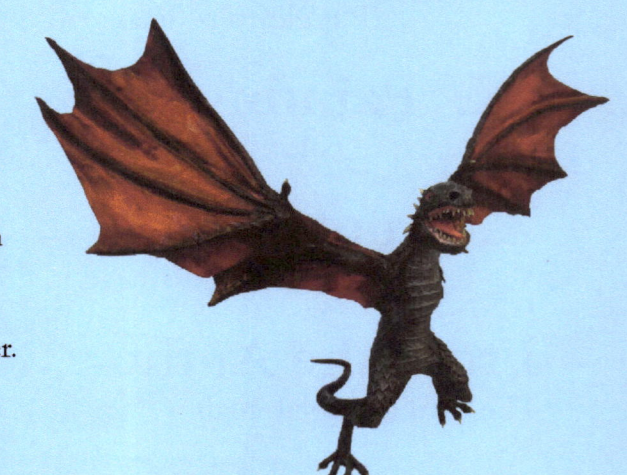

Now you know a little about the "paper mache" we will be doing. Before we start I want to offer a few pieces of advice.

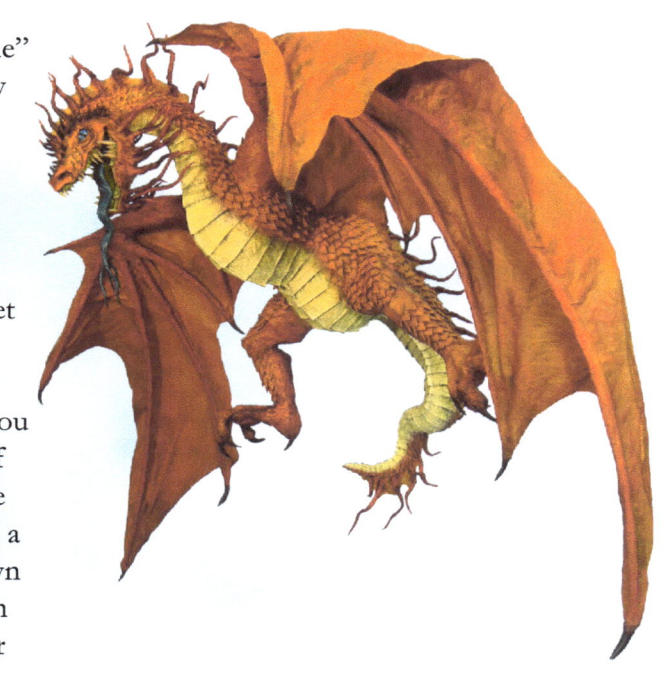

First, you will have more fun if you approach this task loosely. Let your dragon evolve in a natural way. Don't worry if the pieces you make don't look exactly like mine. Use this book as a guide, but don't let it keep you from innovating as you go. Stray from the instructions. Unlike other art forms, this one is very forgiving. If you don't like the way something looks, you can always change it. For example, add an extra pair of arms if you want. I'm going to show you how to make a Wyvern, a particular type of dragon that has legs and a pair of arms that serve as wings (like the dragons shown in this introduction). Add extra arms to make a dragon like the one on the back cover of the book. Make your dragon bigger or smaller. Add extra horns, or not. I can't show you every permutation of the elements that constitute a dragon. So I trust that you will extend the ideas in this book to create a dragon that is uniquely your own. Of course it's okay if you follow the steps exactly. The point is, be bold, be brave. Put yourself into your dragon.

Second, watch some of my time-lapse videos and read some of my blog posts. Use them to augment these instructions. Even if you've already done these things, do them again after reading this book. The videos will appear to slow down. You will see things that you didn't see before. Some of the steps in the book will be clearer after seeing them in motion. Certainly, if you get stuck, contact me. I'm always happy to help (see "From the Author" in the back of the book).

Finally, expect a little frustration, particularly if this is your first paper mache project. I've been making dragons for a very long time. Yet I still find parts of the process to be very challenging. Some of the steps are easy to understand, but that doesn't mean that they are easy to do. I always have trouble draping the wings with cloth. I have to work at it. Speaking of which, I also have to say that this project involves a significant amount of time and effort. There are times when I just don't want to add any more scales. But trust me, every bit of time and effort will be worth it in the end. At the point where you want to throw your dragon in the basement to finish later, DON'"T. Finish it now. Stick with it. Persevere. The rewards will be great. You will LOVE your dragon. You will think that it is better than mine.

Of course your family will think you are crazy in the beginning. Then they will want your dragon when you are done. You will be torn. You love them, and your dragon. It's gonna be tough. Just sayin'.

To my helpers - Eddy who is always underfoot; Max who is always on the newspaper; and very old Riley who used to help, but now doesn't know how she ended up in the bathtub.

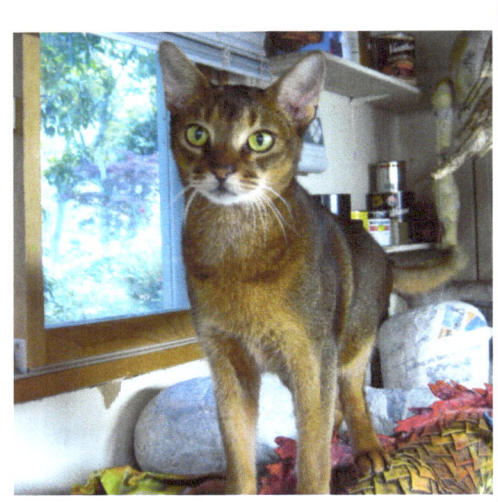

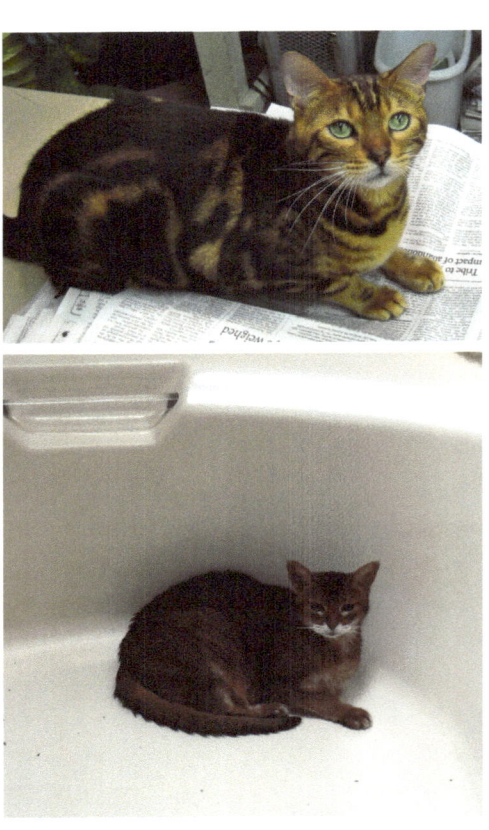

What You Will Need

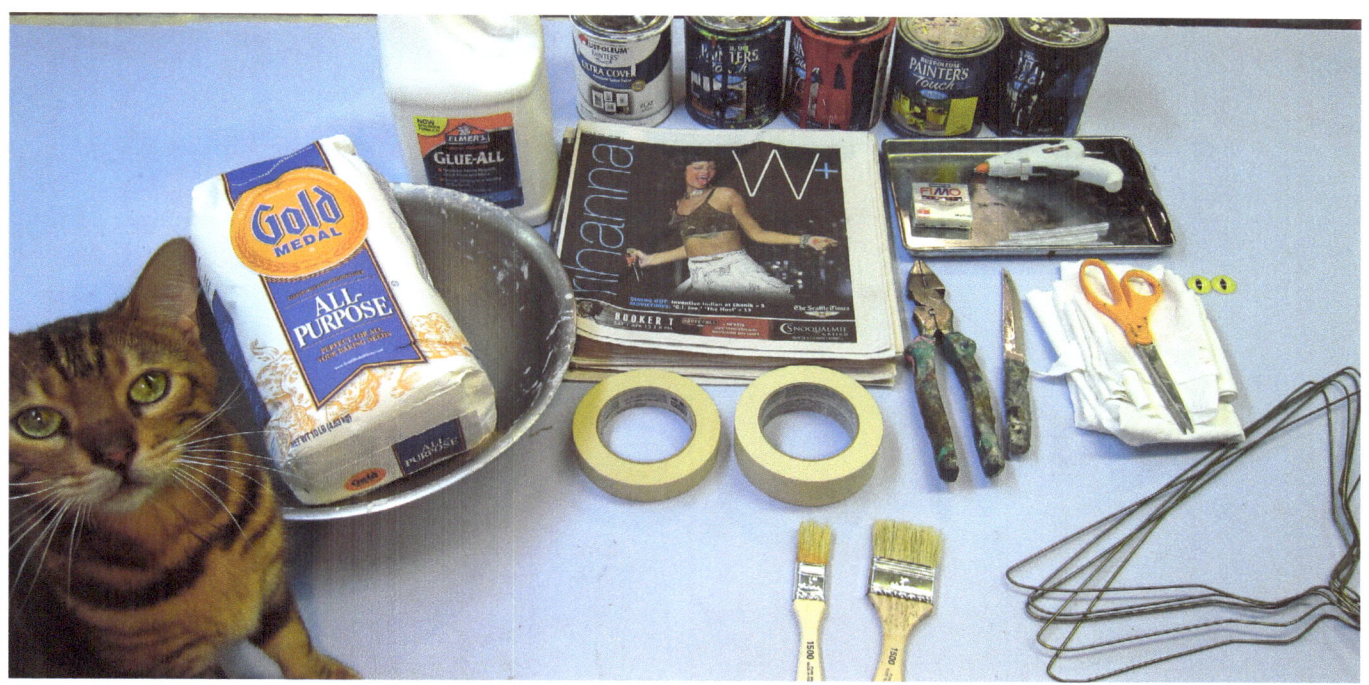

Materials
- 8 inch stack of newspaper
- 1 roll wide masking tape (1½ inch)
- 1 roll thin masking tape (1 inch)
- 7 wire clothes hangers*
- Cheap white flour
- Polymer clay**
- 1 old bed sheet (the older the better)
- 2 quarts of white glue
- All purpose paint***
- Something round for the eyes****

Tools
- Serrated knife (like a steak knife)
- Scissors
- Wire cutters
- Bowls for paste and glue
- Baking sheet
- Hot glue gun
- 1 wide paint brush (1 inch or more)
- 1 thin brush

- A little "helper" named Max or Eddie

* You can get these from friends and family, dry cleaners, thrift stores, and online. But any heavy gauge wire will work.
** All hobby supply stores carry polymer clay. Brands include Fimo and Super Sculpy. "Cold Porcelain" also works well. It is a home-made product, basically corn starch and white glue.   Recipes abound online.
*** Any paint will work although I try to avoid oil-based paints.   Just go to your local hardware store and look for "all purpose" paints. You can usually buy small sample sized amounts of paint for a few bucks. While the small tubes of bright acrylic paints are expensive, you can use those to augment cheaper paints.
**** I like glass eyes. Search "glass eyes taxidermy" online. You will find many companies that sell eyes.   However, anything spherical will work. Clear marbles work wonderfully. Porcelain drawer pulls are great. You can make excellent eyes by rolling polymer clay into balls. You really don't need to buy specialty eyes.

I. Body Parts

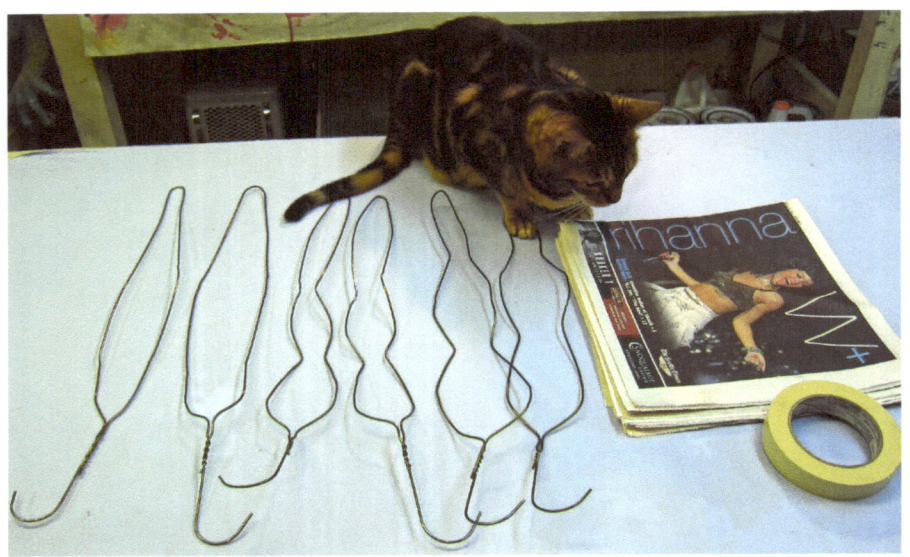

We will start by making the basic body parts: a body, head, legs and arms (in this case, wings), along with a neck and tail. We will crumple paper first, then add the paper mache. My cats love to read the newspaper. I caught Max looking at Rihanna. I'm sure it was the leopard skin top.

You will need:
- **6 wire clothes hangers**
- **A roll of masking tape**
- **A small stack of paper**

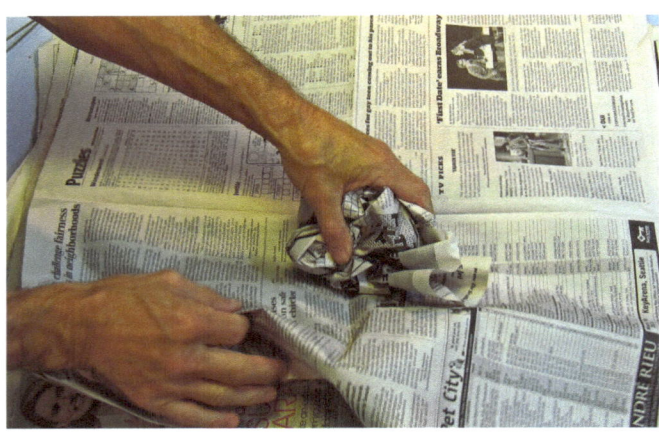

1 Unfold your newspaper. Crumple sheets of paper ONE sheet at a time....

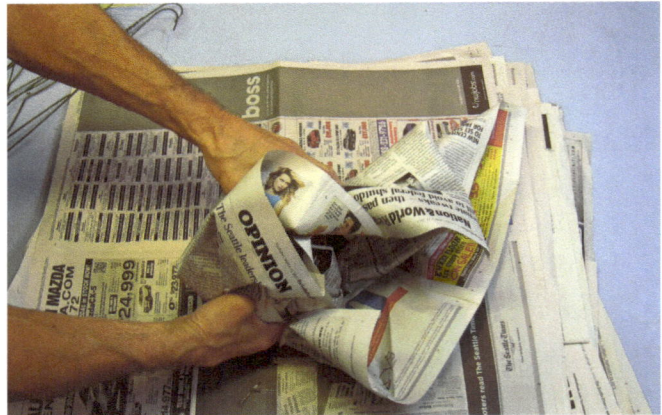

2 ...one over the other...

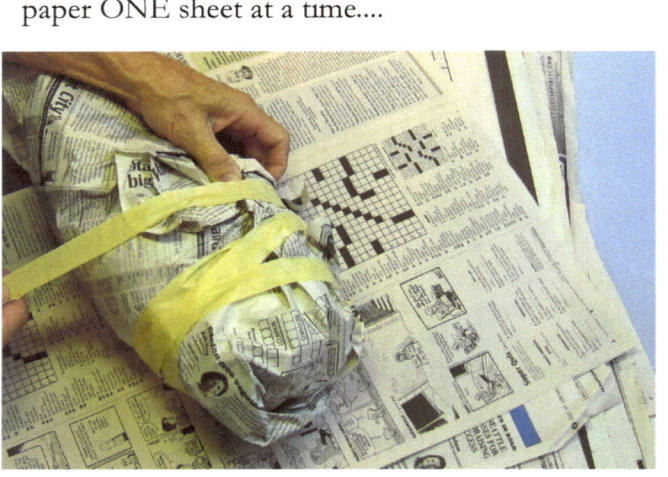

3 ...until the wad of paper is "body sized." How big is that? Eight to ten sheets for this dragon. Of course this can vary. Generally speaking when the wad of paper starts to become a bit unwieldy, then it is about the right size. I'll say this many times. Don't worry too much about whether your ball looks exactly like the one in the photo. Everything will work out fine. Note that my wad of paper is more oblong than spherical. It looks kind of like a big football. I got this shape by pushing down on the center a little more than on the edges.

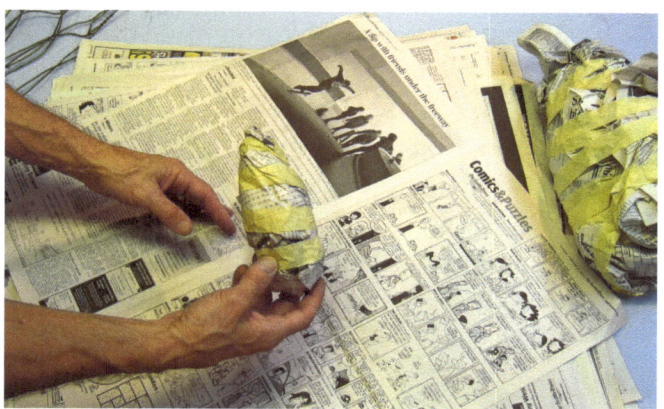

4 Crumple another smaller wad of paper for the head. I make it a little pointed on one end by compressing and twisting the paper. I'm not sure what to call this shape. I use this shape often as you will see. I used three sheets of paper for this head. I always crumple a few extra balls at this point to use for sculpting later. You should too.

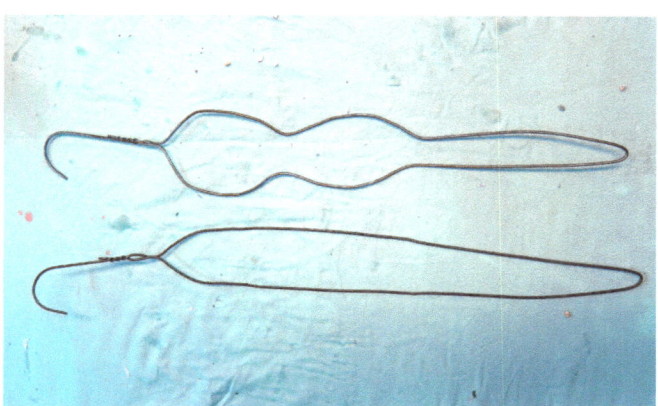

5 I use clothes hangers inside the appendages. I put wads of paper into these hangers and wrap with tape. They provide strength where you need it, in the elbows and knees, and they insure that everything stays put when you bend them into various positions. Bend 2 arms and 2 legs into the figure "8"-ish shape you see in the photo. I make the 8 a little bigger for legs. Then bend 2 hangers into the loop-ish shape for a neck and tail. (See the photo with Max on the opposite page.)

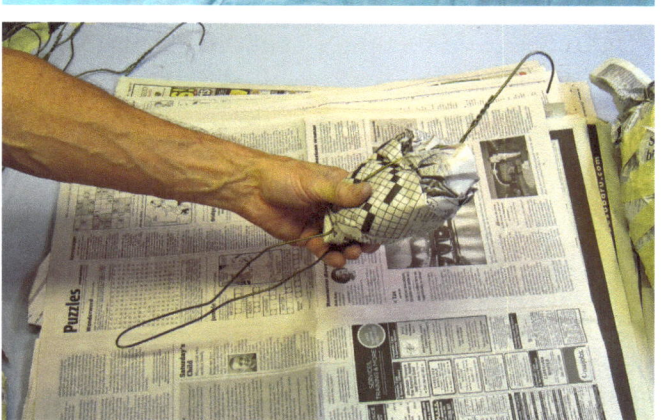

6 Make a thigh that looks like the head. Keep track of how many sheets you use and use the same number on the second leg. Like the head, I used three sheets to make this thigh. Stuff this into the upper part of the figure 8 you made for the legs. Wrap with masking tape.

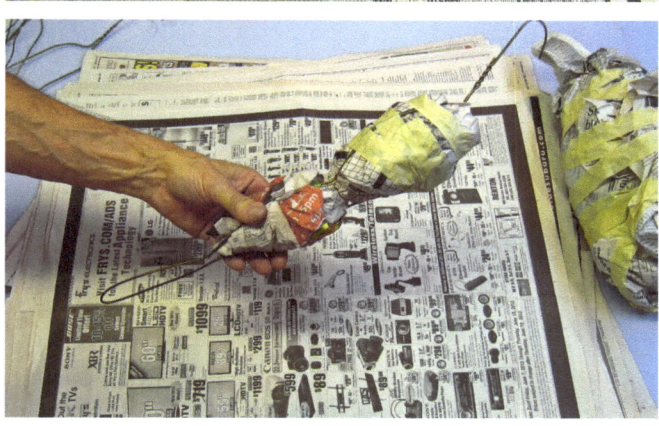

7 Do the same thing for the calf. Crumple, stuff, and wrap with tape. Since I used three sheets for the thigh, I decided to use two sheets for the calf. Of course you can make the legs and arms any size you like. As long as you crumple more sheets for the thighs than for the calves, everything will look great. Finish both legs.

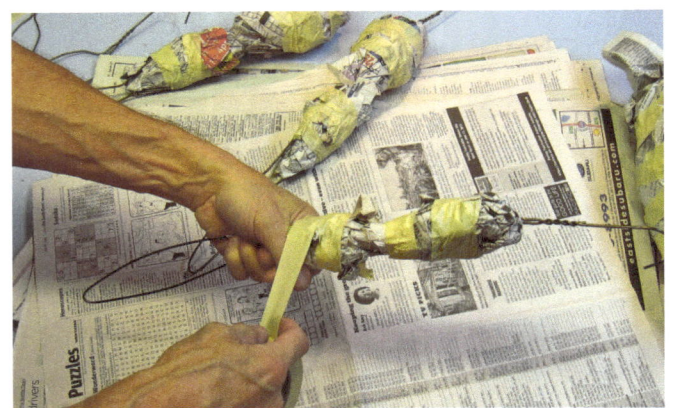

8 Make arms the same way as you made the legs. Just make them a little smaller. Since I used three sheets then two on the legs, I used two sheets for the upper arms and one for forearms. Because I'm making a Wyvern, these arms will actually be the wings. Obviously, if you want to make a dragon with arms **and** wings, you will want to make a second pair of arms at this point.

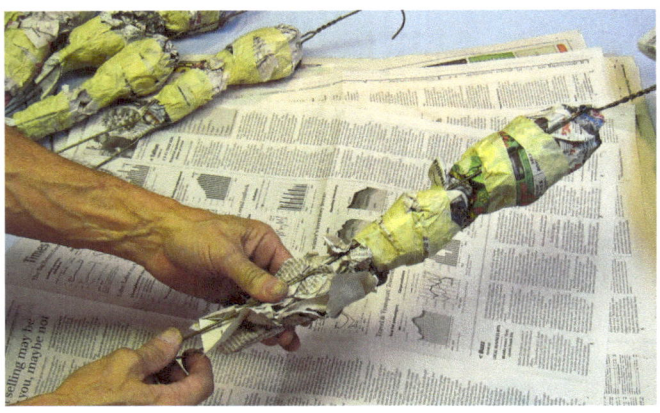

9 Use the clothes hanger loops to make the neck and tail. Crumple and stuff just like you did for the arms and legs. To get a taper I crumpled two sheets of paper for the top, one for the middle, and a half sheet for the bottom.

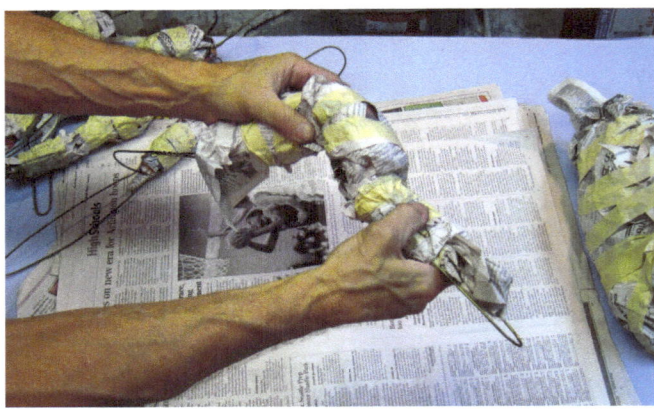

10 I like to add a couple bends in the neck. It gives it more of a serpentine look. If gaps form between the wads of paper as you bend, then stuff a little more paper into them and add more tape.

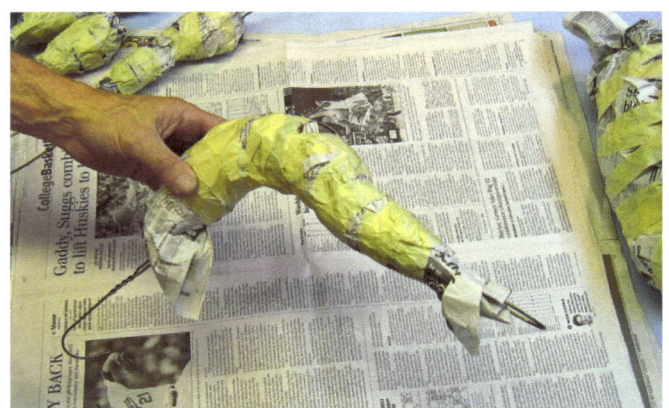

11 Add more masking tape if necessary to fill in the gaps and smooth out the neck.

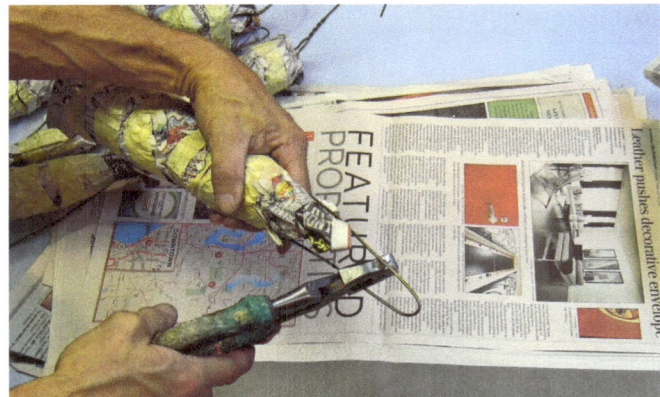

12 Make a tail the same way you made the neck. But you want it to be longer and tapered to a point. To add some length cut one side of the loop toward the end.

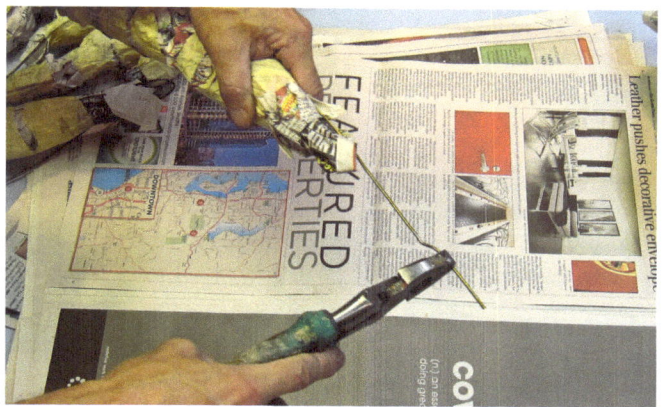
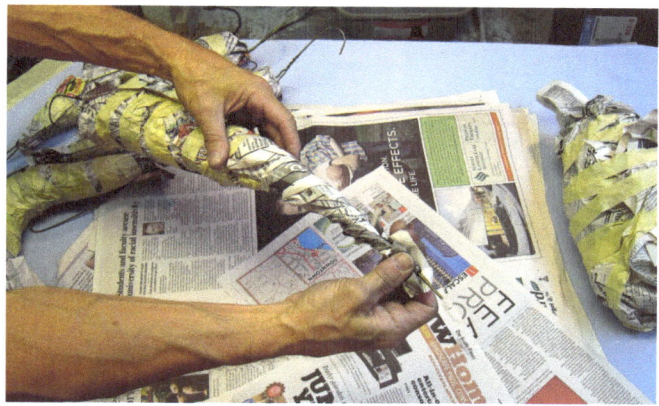

13 Then straighten the wire and twist paper around it. The goal is to get a nicely tapered tail. So I tear pieces of the paper off as I work my way down the wire. It was impossible to get a good photo of this tearing process. This will make sense to you once you start. If you want a longer tail, you can add an additional length of wire. Just tape it to the wire you straightened before you start adding the paper.

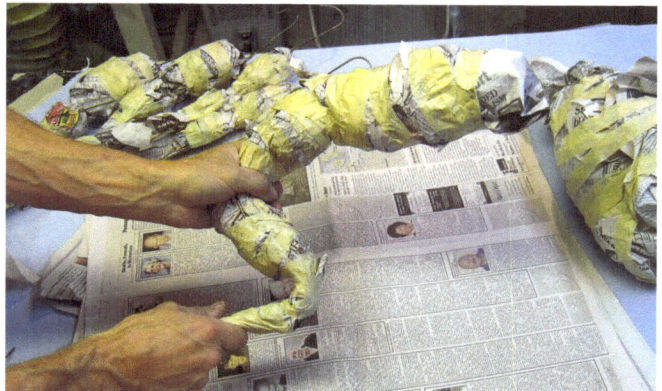
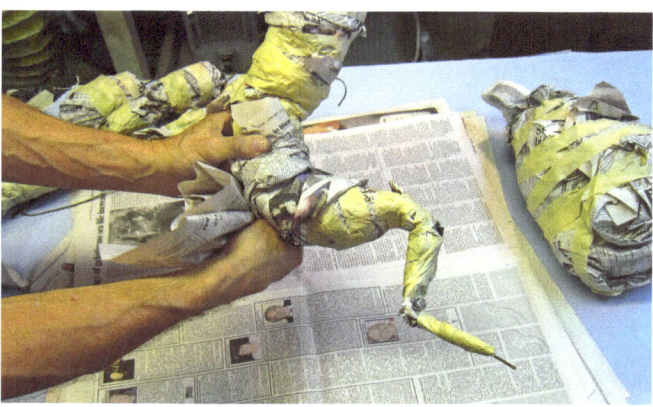

14 As with the neck, this is a good time to add some curves to the tail. You should begin to appreciate wire clothes hangers by now.

15 As with the neck, wrap paper around the tail where gaps appear and add more tape.

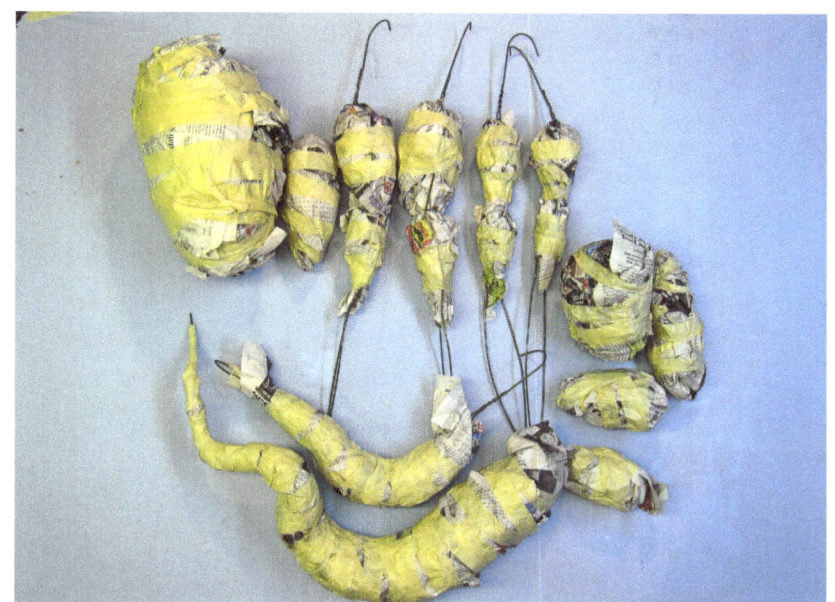

Now you are ready to paper mache the parts. You should have (starting on the left in the photo) a crumpled body, a head, two legs, and two arms. Then (underneath) a neck and a tail. You should also have a few extra balls that you will use when you sculpt (on the right side).

Grab a cookie or two. You worked hard. You need the energy.

II. Paper Mache

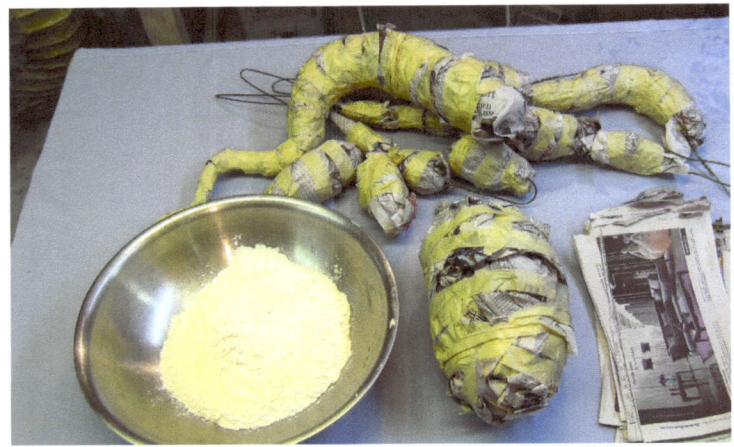

There seem to be as many paper mache paste recipes as there are paper mache artists. They will all work fine, but mine is the correct recipe. Of course those other artists will tell you the same thing. Now, I'm as open minded as the next artist...but mine is the right recipe. I use cheap white flour and water. That's it. Well... I add warm tap water because it feels good. But hey, feel free to experiment. If you want to add salt or baking soda or sugar or powdered milk or tea or anything else to your paste, go right ahead. Feel free to microwave it or heat it on the stove. If you think you've found a better way to make paste, go for it! But please don't write to me to tell me about it. I've heard it all. And my paste is best.

I mix the paste with my hands. No blenders or food-processors. I add enough water to give it the consistency of cream of celery soup. If you want more precision, then the ratio between water and flour is about one-to-one. However, the paste will get thicker as you work; and, because of that, you'll want to add more water as you go. There is just no way to adhere to a strict ratio.

Okay, so listen up. This is very important. When adding the paper strips, put ONLY YOUR HANDS in the paste, not the paper! Attempts to squeegee the excess paste after dipping paper in the paste never work. The paste gets unevenly distributed. Air pockets form that will undermine the shell. The paper disintegrates. Globs of paste between layers don't dry and start to stink. You have to move out of the house. You get the idea. Put only your hands in the paste.

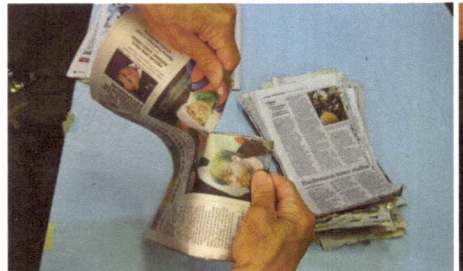
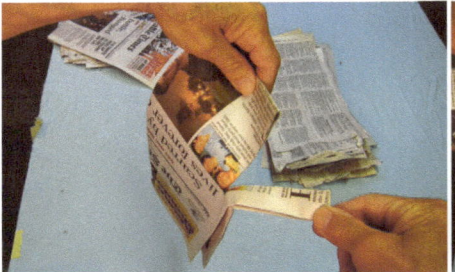
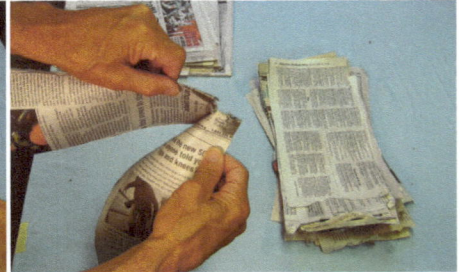

16 Speaking of paper strips, we don't want teeny-weeny ones. A quarter sheet of a newspaper is perfect. Grab a section of newspaper with the fold at the top. Tear it down the middle. Then tear it again next to the folded edge of the section. Recycle the little strip. There is a grain in the newspaper that will help you tear straight.

17 Then find the middle of the section (the pages will tend to fall open to this spot) and tear along the fold. Make a nice stack (at least 2 inches thick) of these strips of paper.

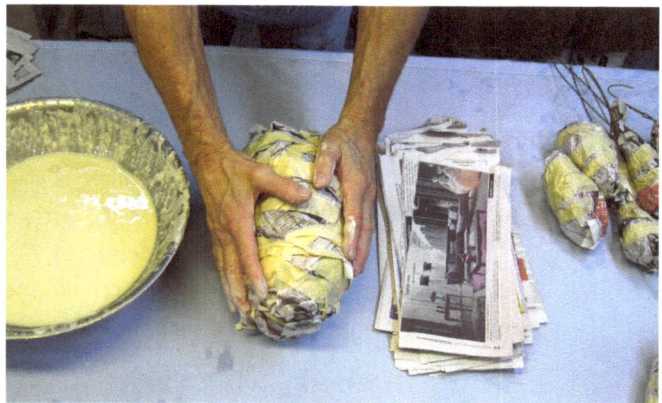

18 Mix the paste. Get your hands VERY wet with paste and rub it over the ball.

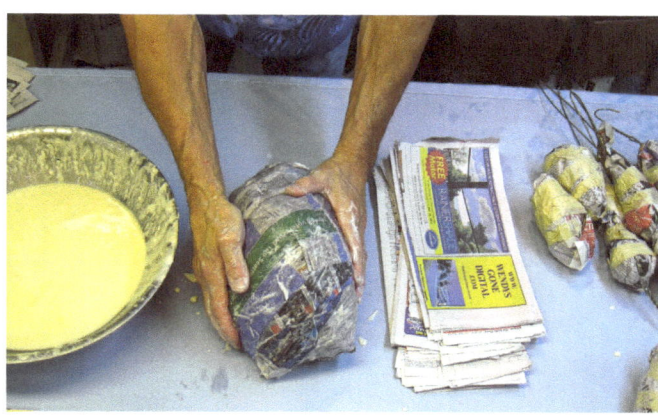

19 Add ONE sheet at a time to the ball. Again, keep your hands really wet. That will insure that the paper gets thoroughly soaked. Add another sheet when the previous one is completely wet.

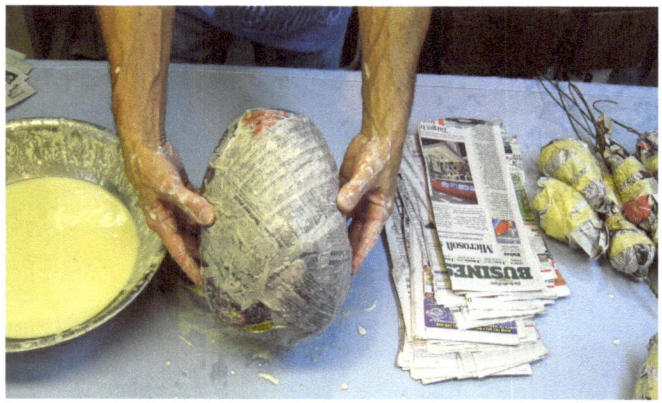

20 Work your way around the body until you have maybe 5 or 6 layers. It's hard to know how many layers you have. Don't worry. You will get a feel for how thick it should be.

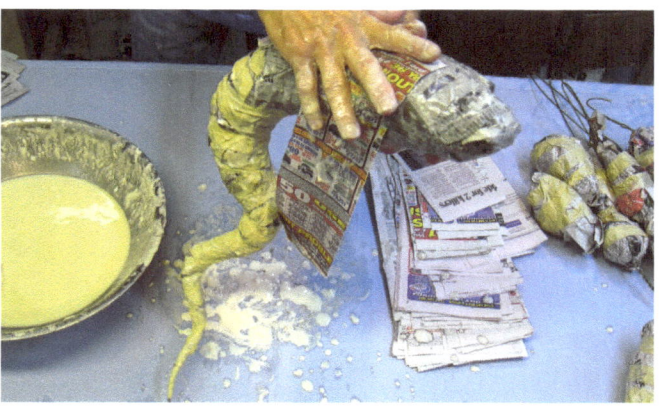

21 Start at the top of the tail or neck. Wrap the paper strips around the appendage working your way to the bottom. Remember, keep your hands very wet and **only** your hands go in the paste!

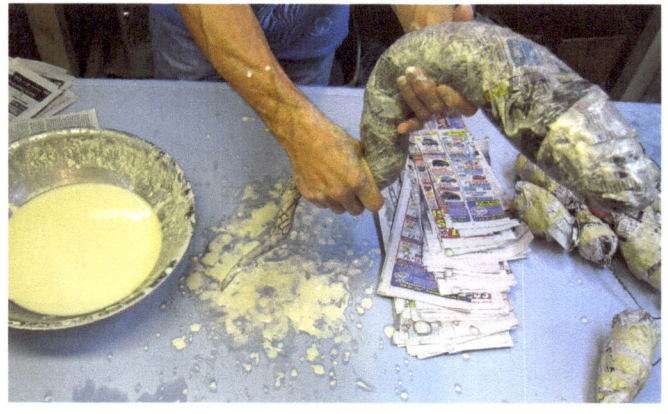

22 Squeeze the appendage as you work. This will force out air bubbles and build in a little tension, making everything nice and smooth.

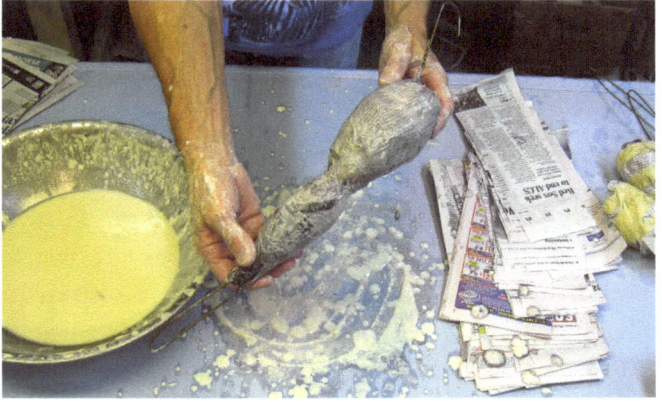

23 Repeat this process for the arms and legs. Put these someplace warm to dry. Use the hooks to hang them, which will accelerate the drying.

III. Little Appendages

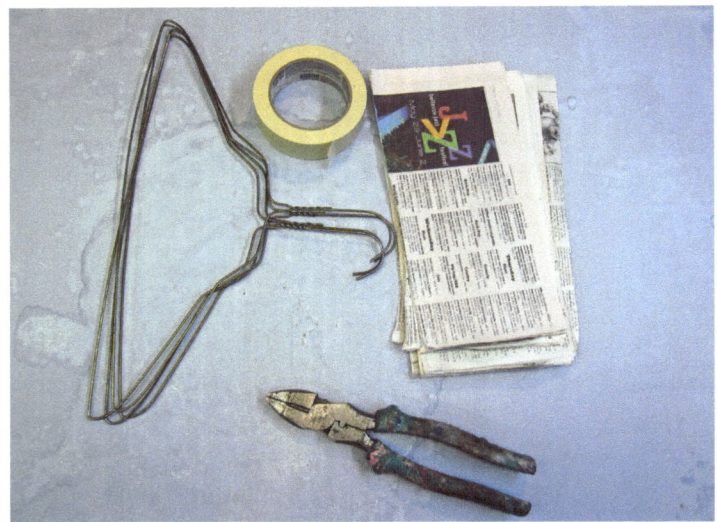

A dragon needs fingers and toes, and usually a tongue. You might also want horns or tentacles and spines for the back. I make all of these by twisting paper around pieces of clothes hanger and wrapping with tape. Once again, the wire allows you to bend these into any shape you want.

> **You will need:**
> - **Clothes hangers**
> - **Heavy duty wire cutters**
> - **Masking tape**
> - **Newspaper strips**

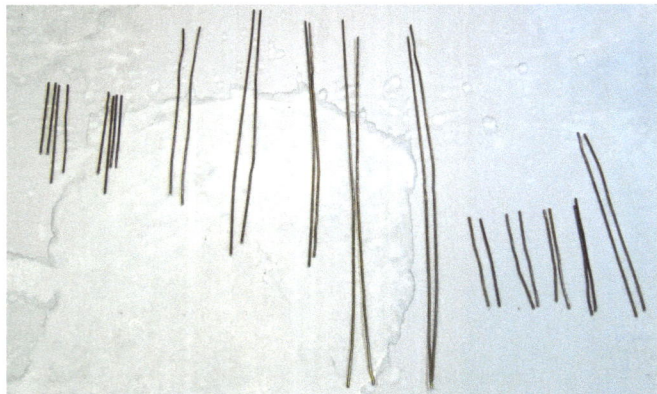

24 Cut pieces of hangers into the approximate lengths listed below. You can always trim them later. From left to right in the photo:

For little **Ears**: Cut 8 pieces around 2 inches long.
For the "fingers" in the **Wings**: Cut 2 around 7 inches, 4 around 12 inches, and 4 around 16 inches.
For **Toes**: Cut 8 pieces around 3½ inches long.
For a **Tongue**: Cut 2 pieces around 6 inches long.

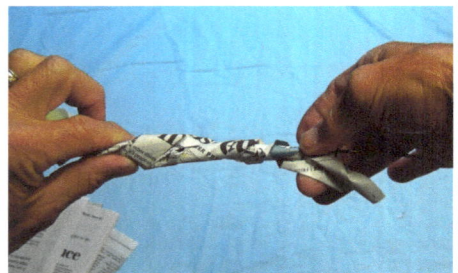
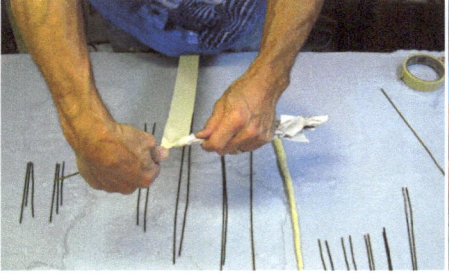
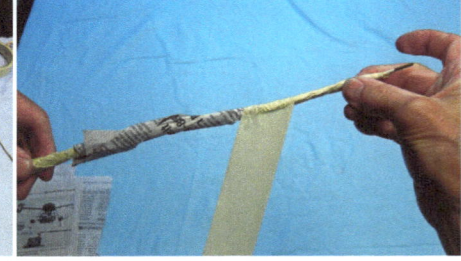

25 Think of a bat's wing. It is essentially leather draped between long fingers (in two parts, the metacarpals and phalanges). That's the model I use for Wyvern wings. We'll start by making these "fingers," the long ones first. Use the paper strips left over from doing the paper mache for these. Pinching the edge of a strip of paper against the hanger (so it doesn't move), wrap and twist the paper around the wire (in a motion up and away from your body). I add a taper by twisting the paper tighter as I work my way down the wire. This first strip will cover about half the wire. Then I wrap with tape. I put the roll of tape between my legs. I pull on the tape as I turn the finger (in the same up and over direction), keeping it taut.

26 Similarly, twist a second, smaller strip of paper on the wire that is left. Again, twist the paper tighter toward the end to add a taper and bring the finger to a point.

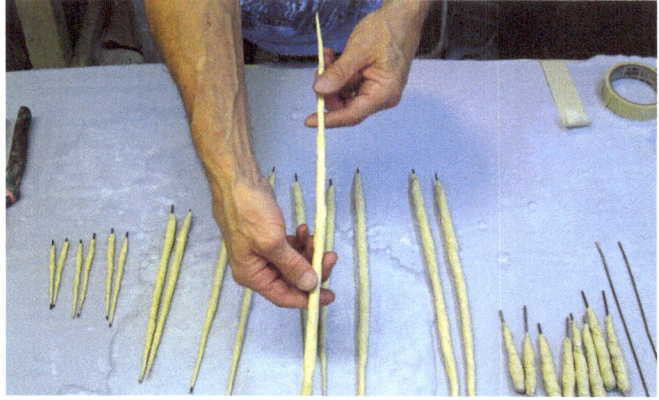

27 Finish all the fingers from long to short. This takes a little practice, particularly with the longest ones. But it will get easier with each finger that you make.

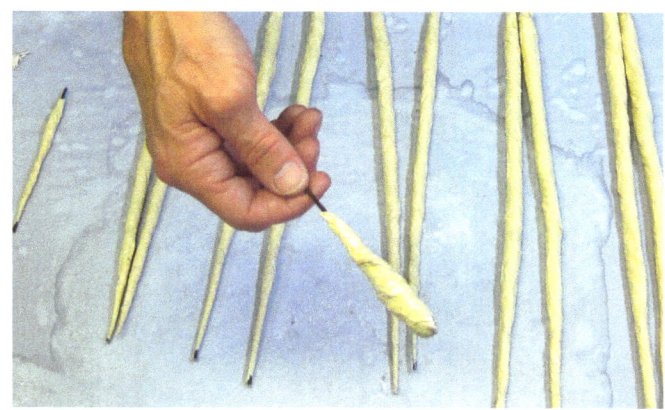

28 Make the toes in the same way. They are just shorter and blunt at the end.

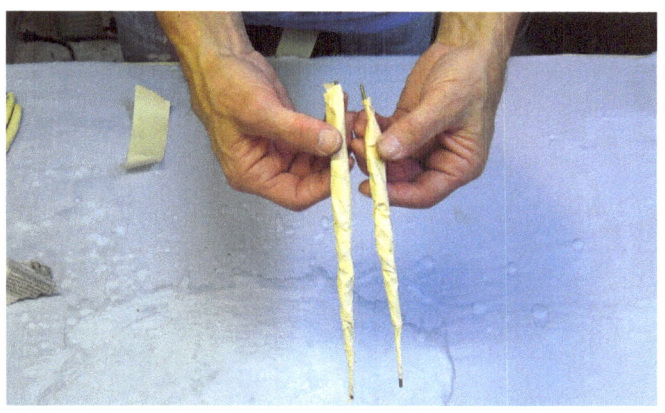

29 I have a great way to make a tongue. Use the two 6 inch pieces of wire. Make two more fingers.

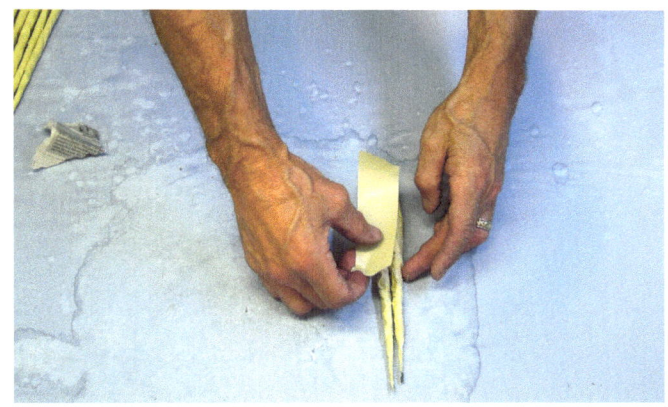

30 Put them next to each other and add a piece of tape on one side only. That will be the underside of the tongue.

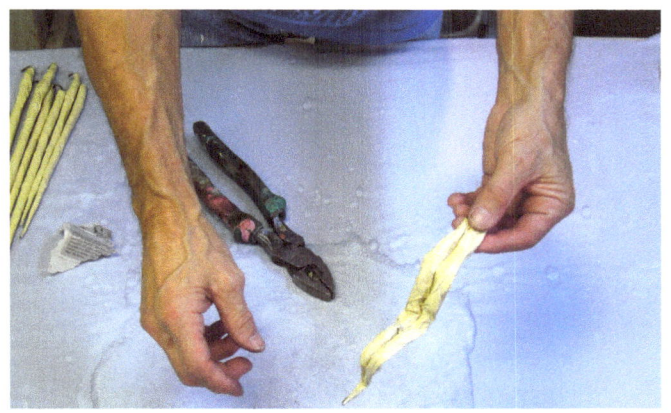

31 Having tape on just the underside preserves the separation of the two pieces. It adds a little valley down the middle so that it looks more like a tongue. Add a few interesting bends.

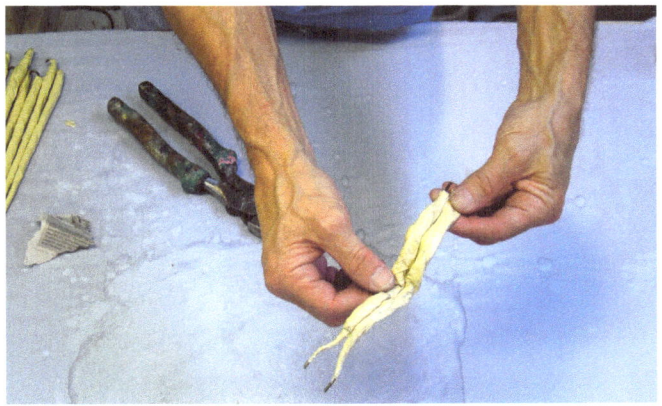

32 You can either leave the tongue pointed at the end or split it into a fork (my preference for this dragon). Just bend the two wires outward at the end.

IV. Jaws, Claws, Teeth and Horns

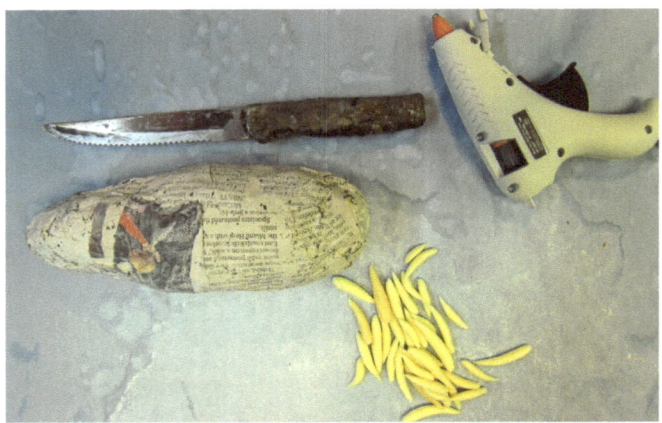

It's always easier to put together and paint the jaws before assembling the rest of the dragon. First, you need teeth. You might as well make the horns and claws while you are at it.

> **You will need:**
> - **Your head-shaped mache ball**
> - **A hot glue gun**
> - **A serrated knife.**
> - **Polymer clay (or equivalent)**

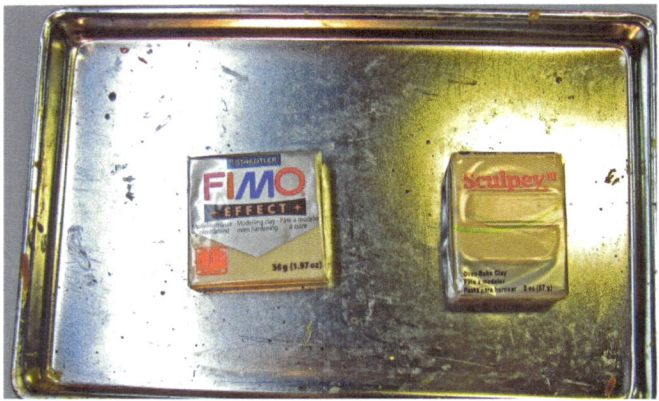

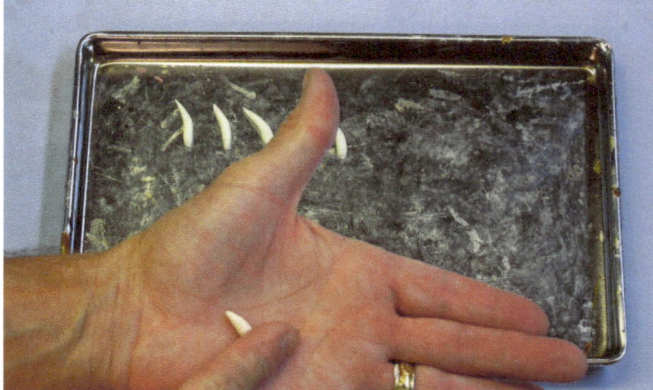

33 I make most of my teeth and claws, and many of my horns, out of polymer clay. You can find several brands at any craft store. This clay is easily shaped and then baked in your oven. You can also use the "Cold Porcelain" I mentioned in the supply list. It is very inexpensive and dries in the air. Whatever you use, pinch off a little bit and roll it with your finger into the palm of your hand. Press a little harder on one end to make a point. I like to add a little curve to these. Claws and teeth have the same basic shape, although claws are usually a little longer.

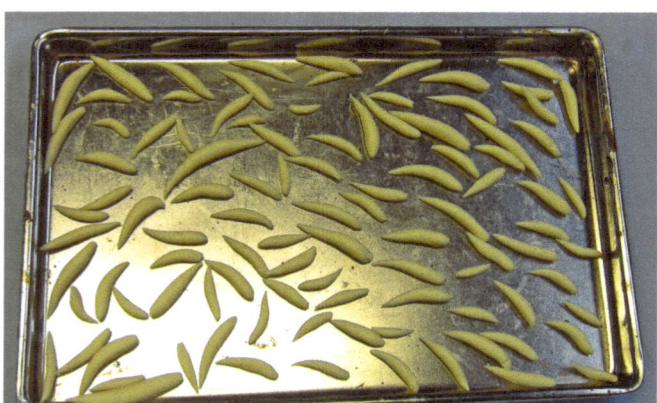

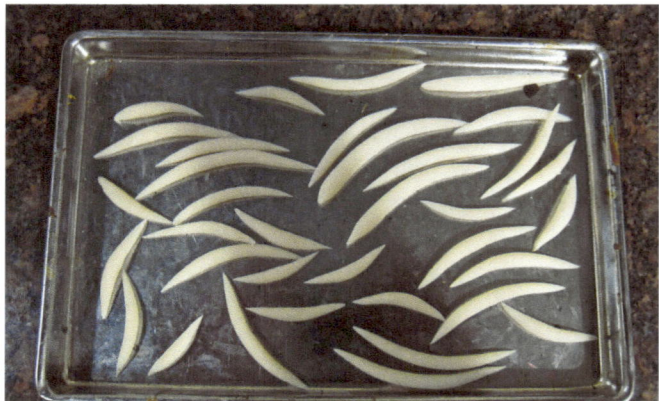

I used about 30 teeth and 10 claws for this dragon. As evidenced by the photo on the left, I always make extra, just in case. **Hint:** Many times I will make longer pieces tapered to a point on both ends (photo on the right). I can then cut teeth or claws or horns of any length from either end.

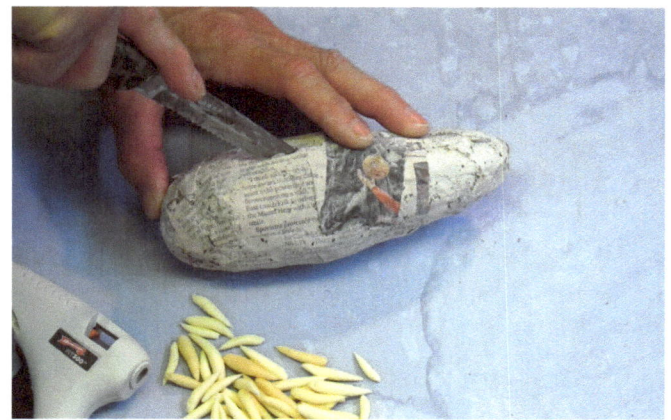

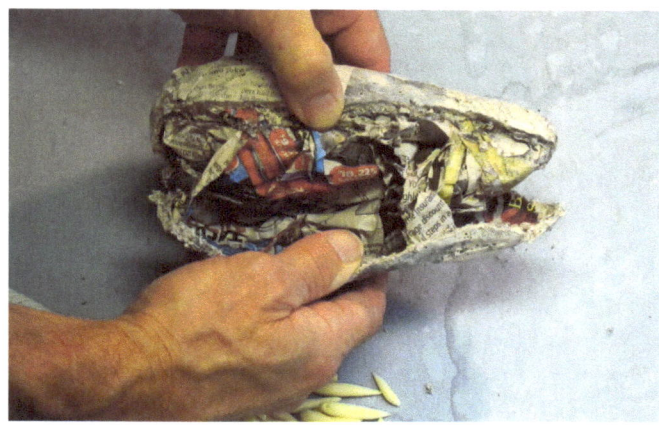

34 To make jaws, slice open the ball with your knife. I don't like straight cuts. A jagged cut makes a better looking dragon jaw. Note that the knife does not have to be sharp. It is the serration that makes the easy cut. It is like using a saw.

35 Pry the ball open and pull out the wad of paper. This will give you two paper mache shells for jaws.

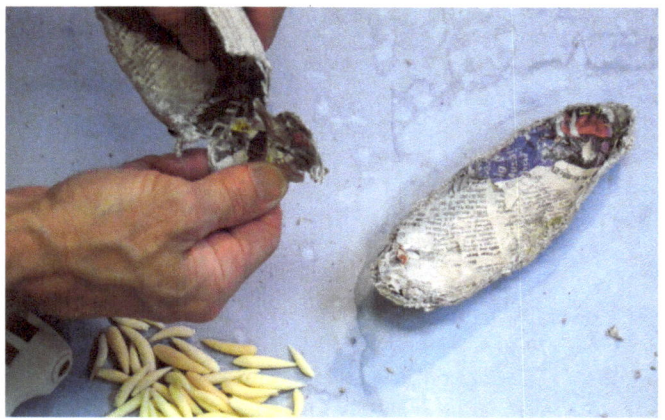

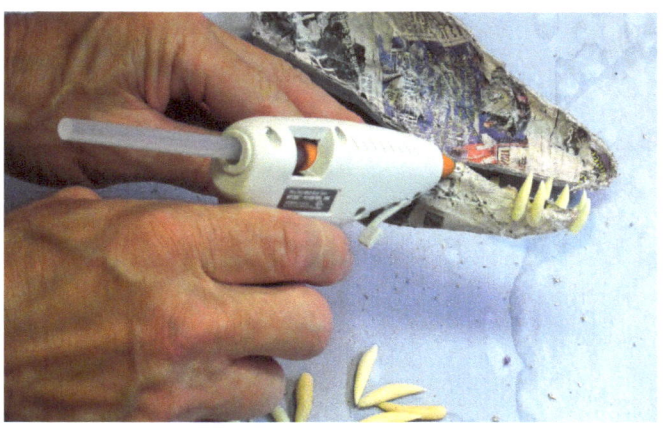

36 Tear out the back of one of these shells to make room for the tongue.

37 Use your hot glue gun to add teeth.

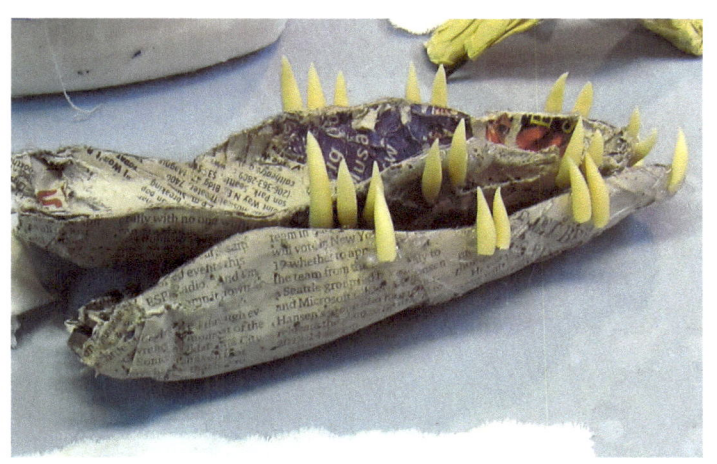

I really like adding teeth in clusters. In this jaw the clusters have two or three teeth. Then I have a couple single teeth in the front. It works well to make the clusters on one jaw match the gaps on the opposite jaw. Of course you can make your mouth any way you like. A full set of teeth on top and bottom looks very menacing. Try larger canines or fangs. Or maybe you want an old, toothless dragon. Experiment until you get the jaws you want (and deserve).

V. Cloth Mache- Part 1

I will talk more about "cloth mache" later. For now, just the basics. I want to add cloth and glue to some pieces before assembling the dragon.

> **You will need:**
> - **An old bed sheet (the older the better)**
> - **Scissors**
> - **White (all purpose) glue**
> - **Your "fingers," jaws, and tongue**
> - **A container to hold the glue.**

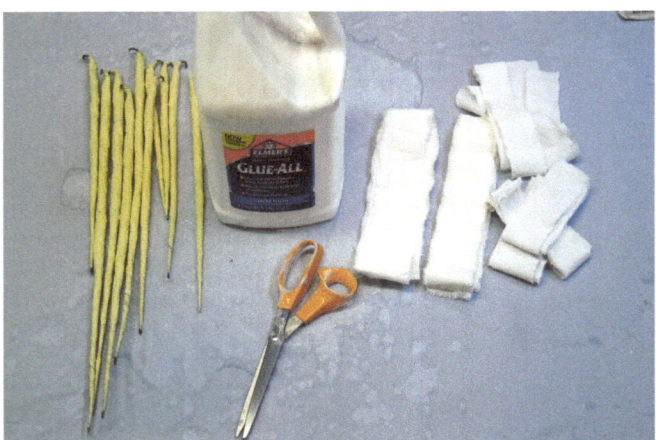

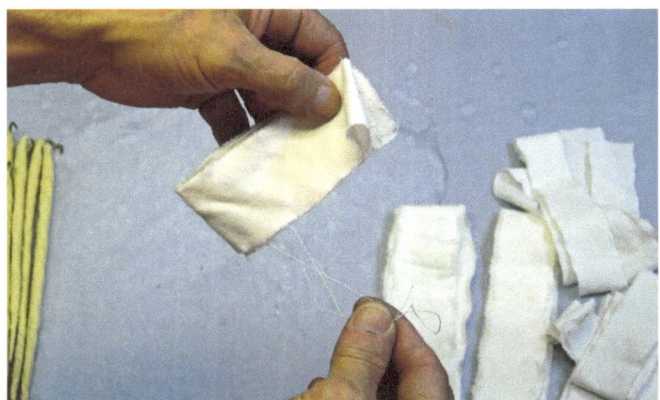

38 To add strength to the wings we will cloth mache the "fingers" we made earlier. Preparing the cloth in advance is important. Tear part of the bed sheet into various sized strips. Fold the strips and pull off the loose strings.

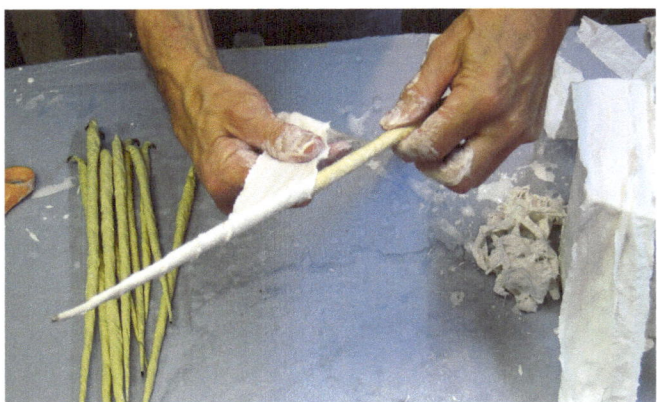

39 These strips are about an inch wide for the fingers. Soak the strips in the glue and squeeze out the excess. Start the cloth at the point and turn the finger while tugging on the cloth. This builds in tension and makes the cloth tight.

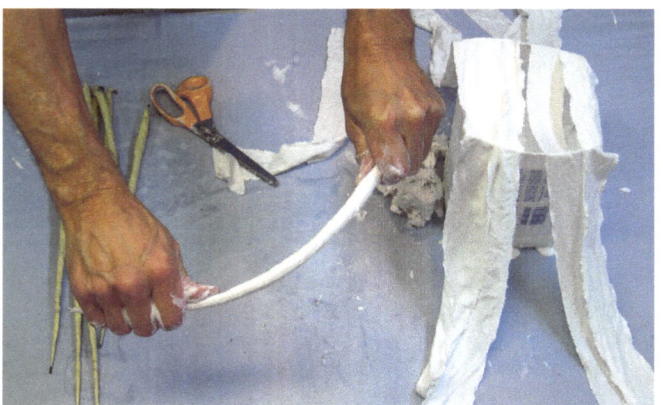

40 After you've worked your way to the bottom, add a little bend in the finger to give the wings some curvature. Hang these someplace warm to dry.

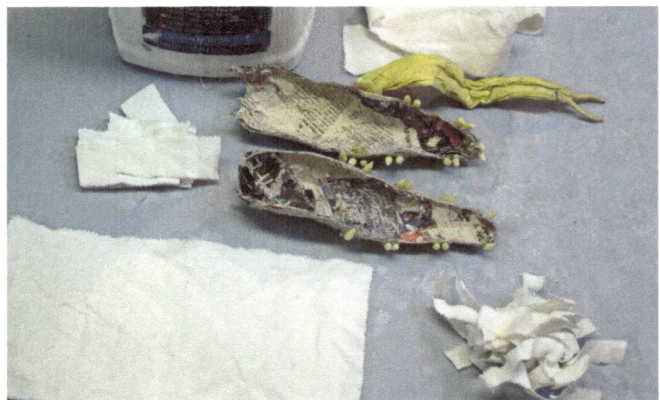

41 Back to the jaws and tongue. Tear some thin strips of cloth (about ½ inch wide) and cut them so that they are about 1 ½ inches long. We will use these to wrap the teeth.

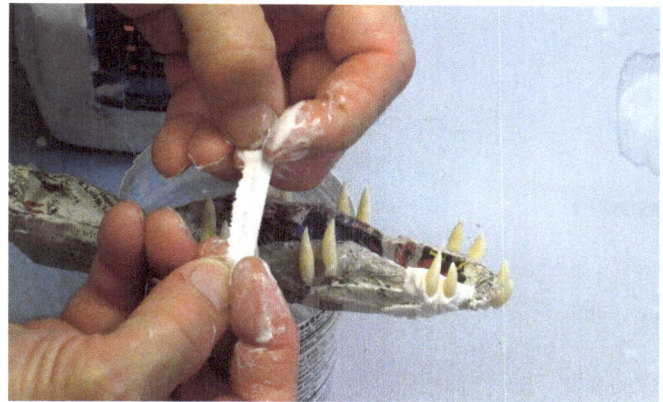

42 Dip a little strip in the glue and fold it lengthwise. This provides a gum line when placed against a tooth.

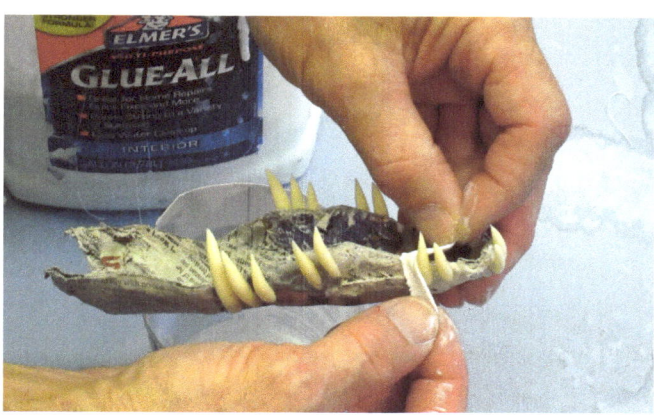

43 Wrap the strip at an angle, across the base of the tooth and onto the shell. Note that the tooth I wrapped is on the outside of a two-tooth cluster.

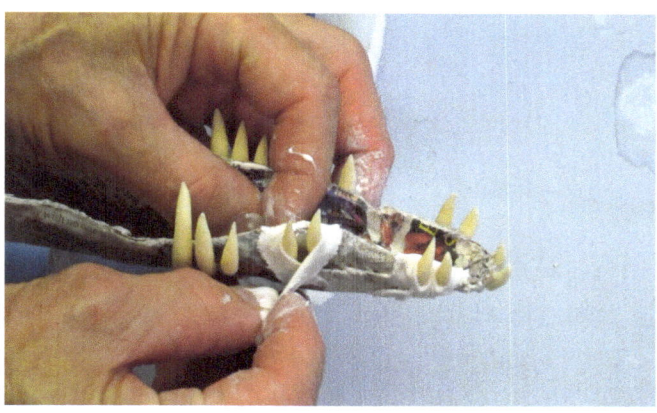

44 Wrap a new strip, angled in the opposite direction, on the outside of this cluster. Fold the next cloth strip on both sides so that you have a fold along both edges.

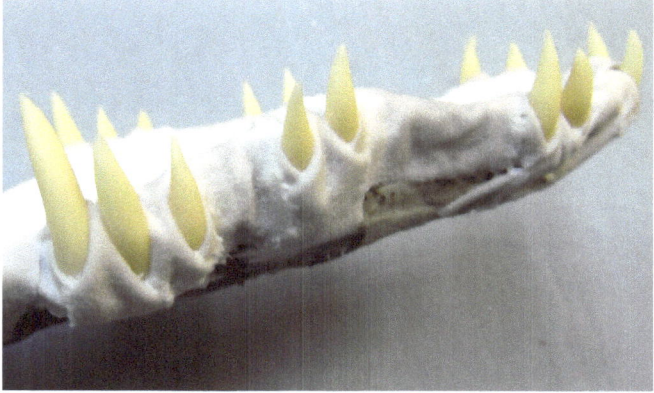

45 Put it between the teeth. The strip will tend to unfold at the ends and blend into the jaw. Similarly, add the cloth strips around all of the clusters of teeth as well as the single, front teeth.

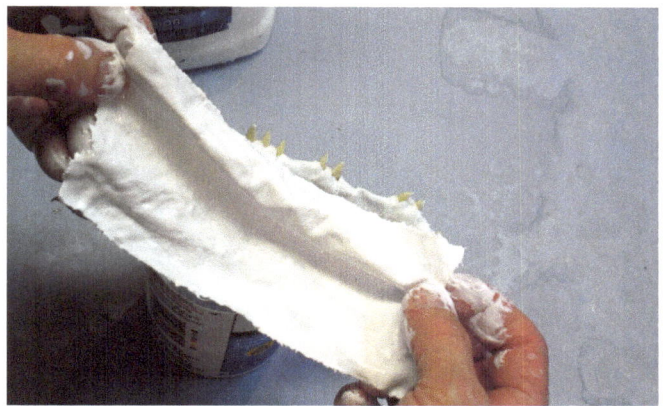

46 After wrapping all of the teeth you will want to cover the roof of the jaw. Use a piece of cloth bigger than the jaw. Dip it in glue and lay it inside.

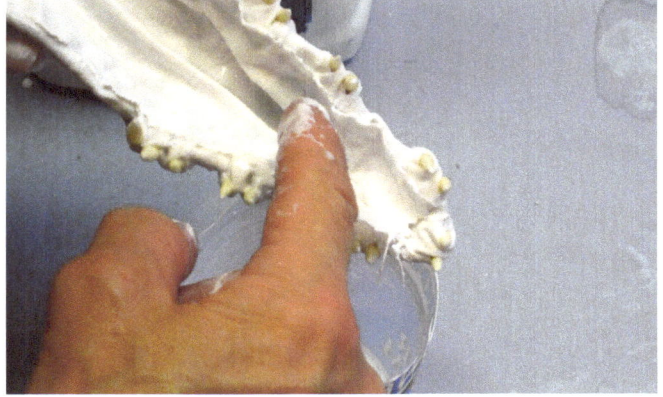

47 Tamp down the cloth at the edges. The excess cloth will form wrinkles, perfect for the inside of a mouth. Cloth mache both jaws.

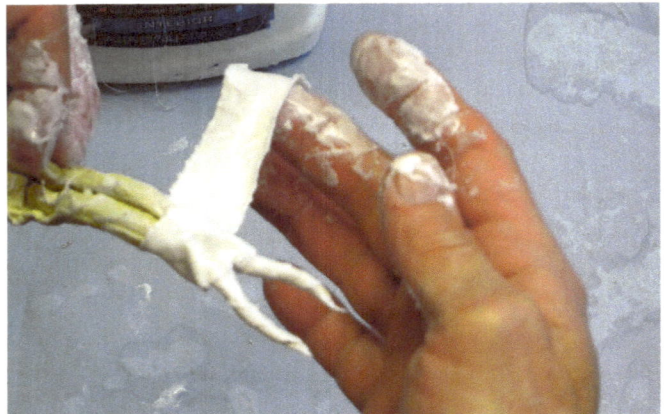

48 For the tongue, wrap small pieces of cloth around the pointed forks. Then use a wider and longer strip of cloth to wrap **loosely** around the entire length of the tongue.

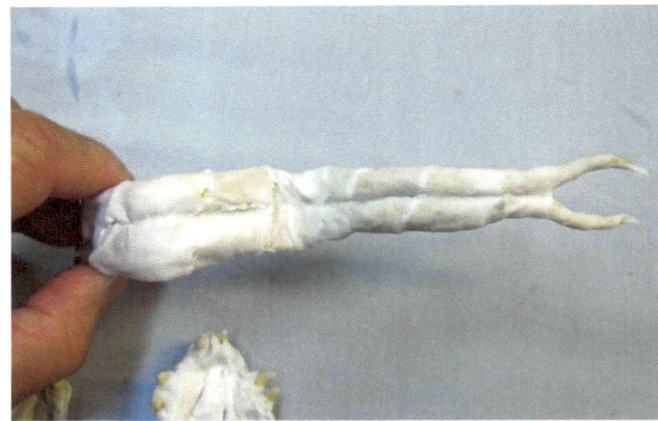

49 Use a knife to press the cloth between the two parts of the tongue. This will accentuate the valley of the tongue. Let all of these pieces dry overnight.

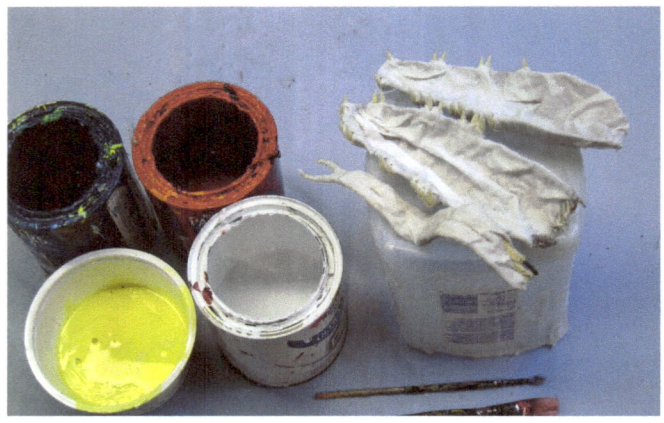

50 I'll talk more about painting later. As I said, we want to paint the jaws early in the process. Gather the colors you'd like to use for the mouth.

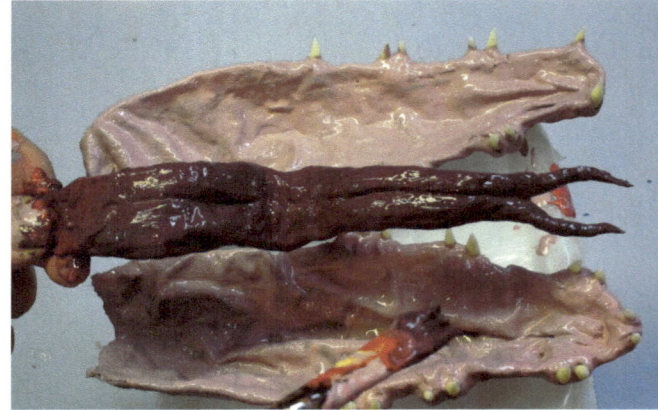

51 I've chosen a pink-ish, purple-ish combination. Paint your jaws and tongue and let them dry. It's okay to get a little paint on the teeth.

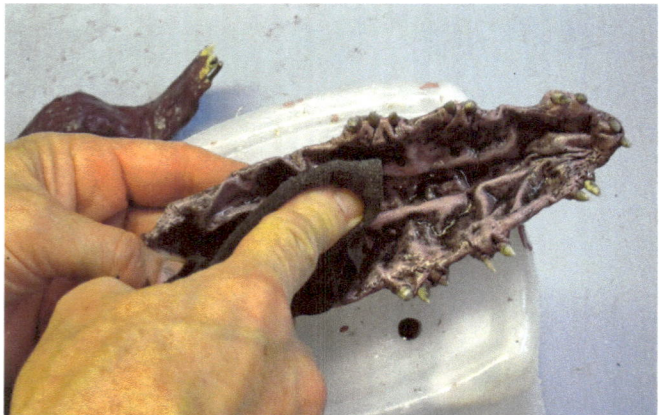

52 I also "blackwash" the jaws at this point. Add water to some black paint. Apply this diluted paint and wipe it off before it dries.

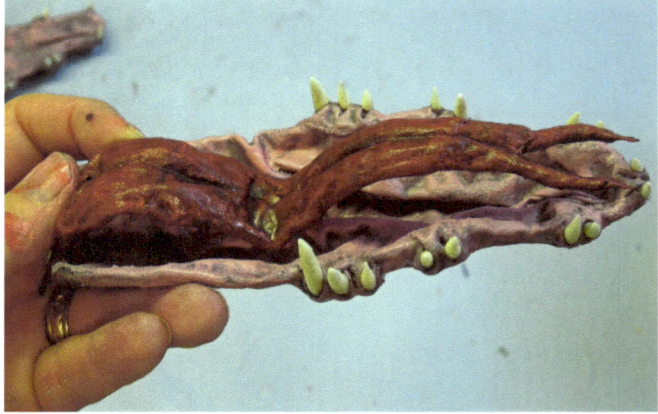

53 Sometimes the blackwashing can end up a little too dark. If it does, add a few highlights. Here I put a little more pink on the high spots of the jaws and some red on the tongue.

VI. Assembly

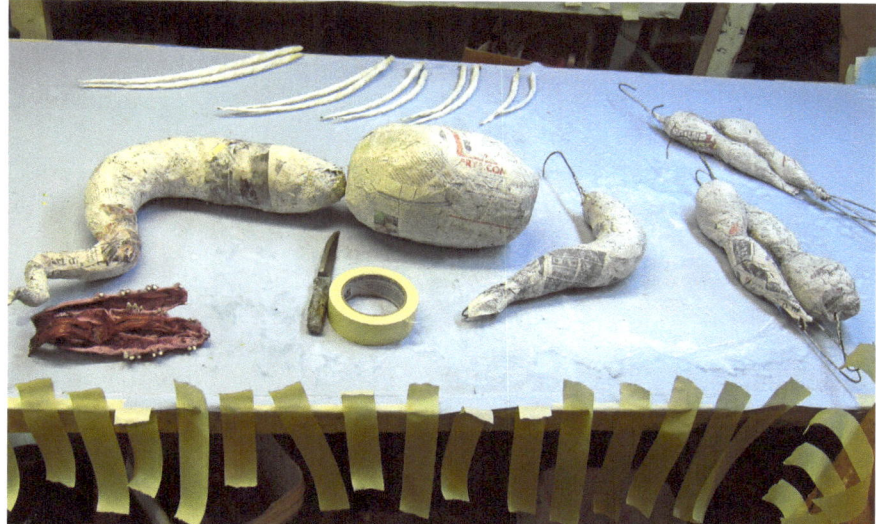

You've been very patient so far. Lots of just making parts. It's good for you, this delayed dragon gratification. But now it's time for the dragon to start taking shape. So hang on to your pants. This is going to be fun.

> **You will need:**
> - **Body parts you made**
> - **Knife and wire cutters**
> - **Tape (wide is best here)**

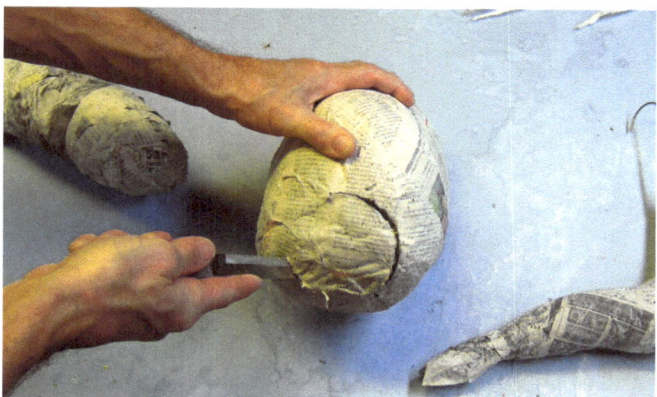

54 We'll add the tail first. Cut a hole at the end of the body. As a general rule, I try to cut the hole a little smaller than the appendage I'm inserting. That way I get a snug fit.

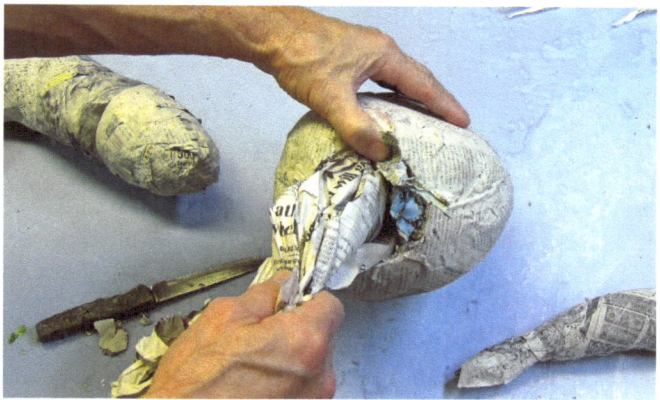

55 While this isn't absolutely necessary, I like to make the dragon lighter by pulling the wads of paper out of body through the hole. Sometimes you have to grab one sheet at a time.

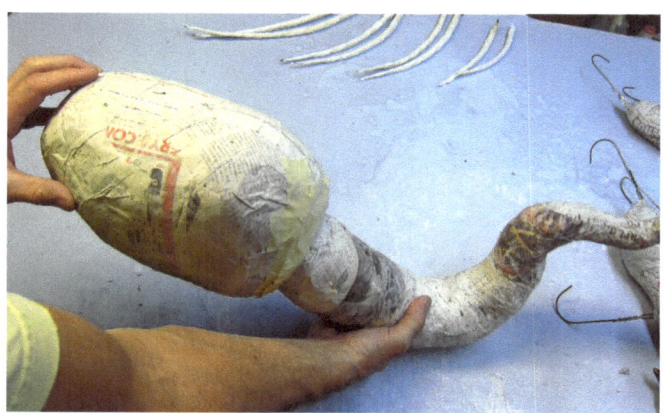

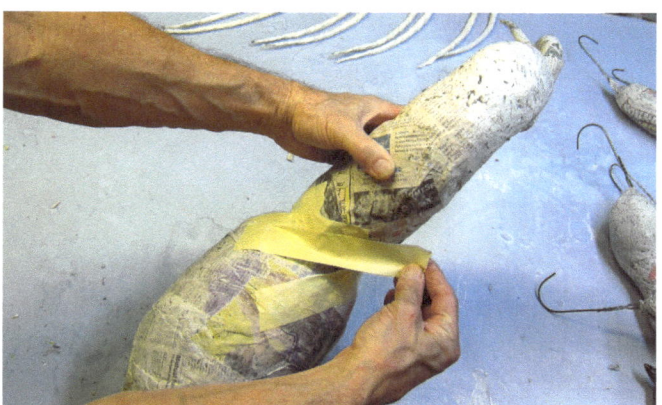

56 Push the tail into the hole you just made. Tape it into place. Some advice....start the tape on the body and pull it at an angle across the tail as you work your way around the base. This will hold the tail tightly in place. In fact, use this taping method whenever you add appendages.

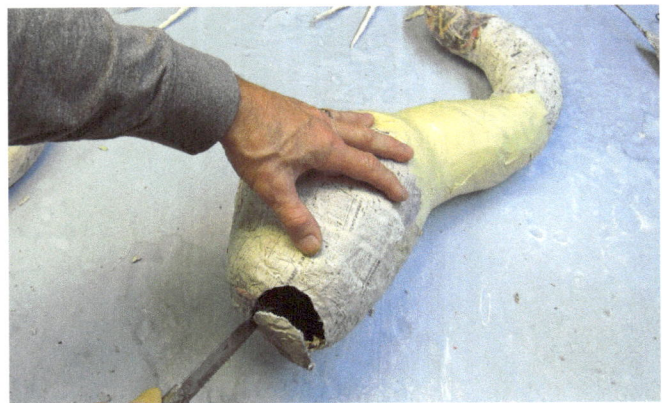

57 Cut a hole at the other end of the body for the neck.

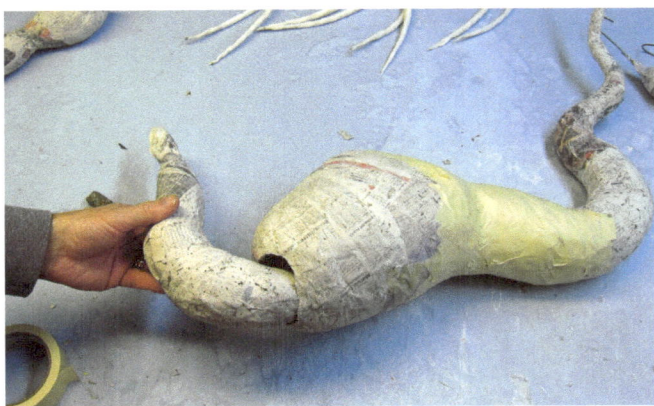

58 Stick the neck into the hole. Note that in this case I made the hole too big. Bummer.

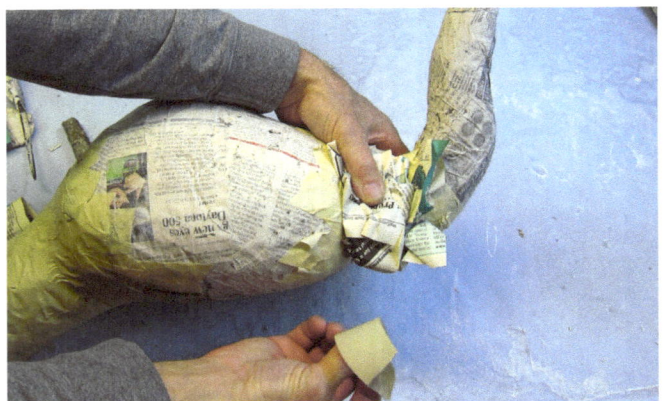

59 Don't worry. Whenever something like this happens just grab a small wad of newspaper and fill the void. Then add tape to hold it in place. Finish taping the neck onto the body. Remember, pull the tape at an angle, and make sure that each piece is firmly patted down.

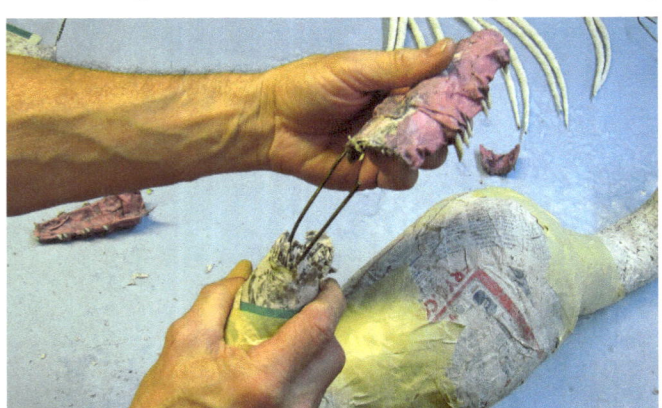

60 Time to put on the head. Expose the wire loop at the end of the neck. Cut the wire in the middle and straighten the two ends. Then push the upper jaw onto the wires so that they go between the outside shell and the cloth mache inside the mouth.

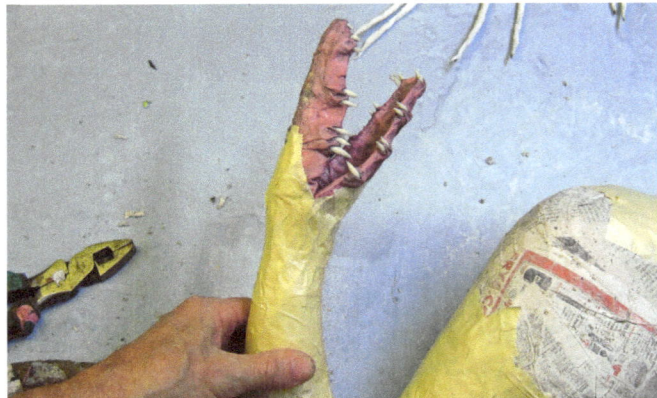

61 Place the lower jaw underneath the top jaw and tape it into place. (No need for wire supports for the lower jaw.)

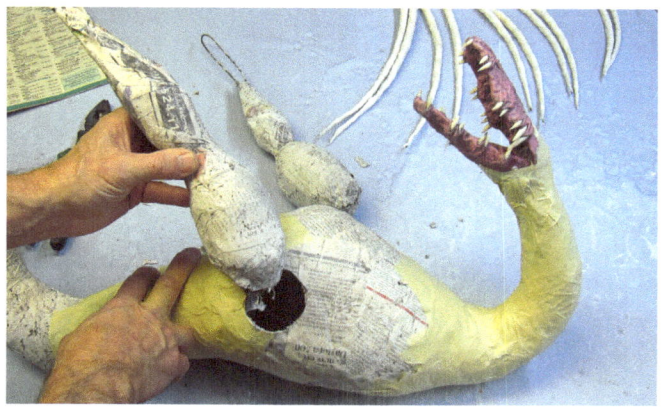 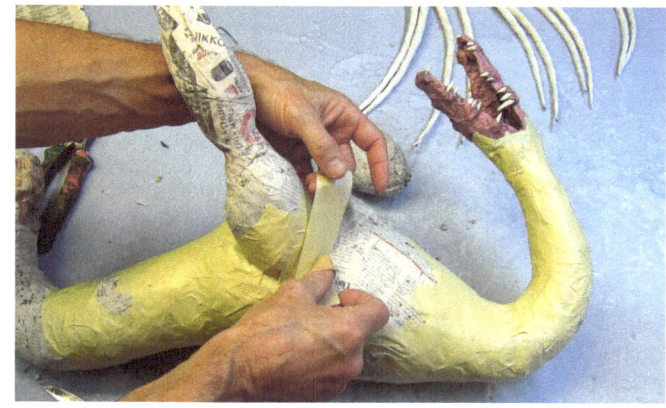

62 Time to attach the legs. Cut a hole on the side of the dragon just in front of the tail and push a leg into it. Secure it with tape as I described earlier. This turned out to be a perfect sized hole. I have a simple test for the perfect hole. If a leg, or any other appendage, stays in place before you add the tape, then the hole is exactly right. Add tape nevertheless.

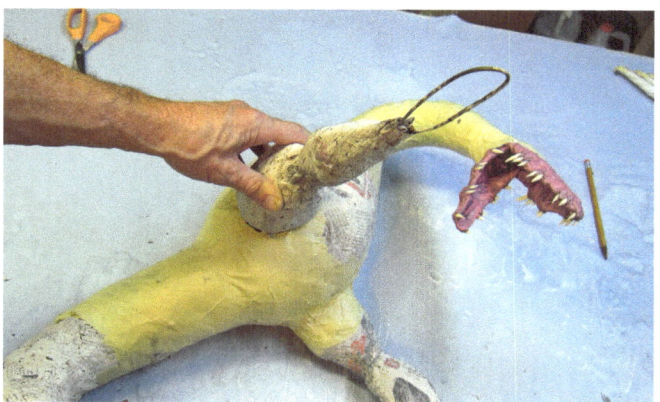 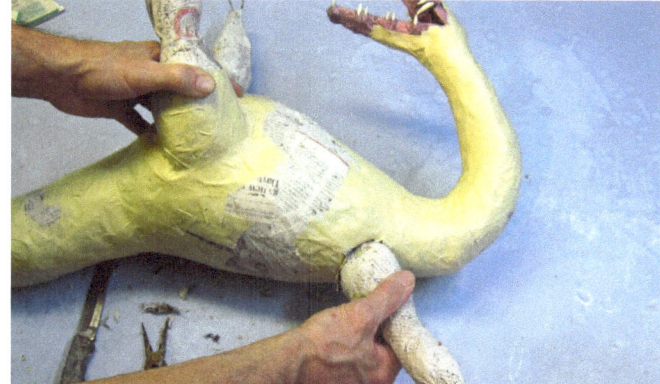

63 Add the other leg.

64 Add the arms at the base of the neck.

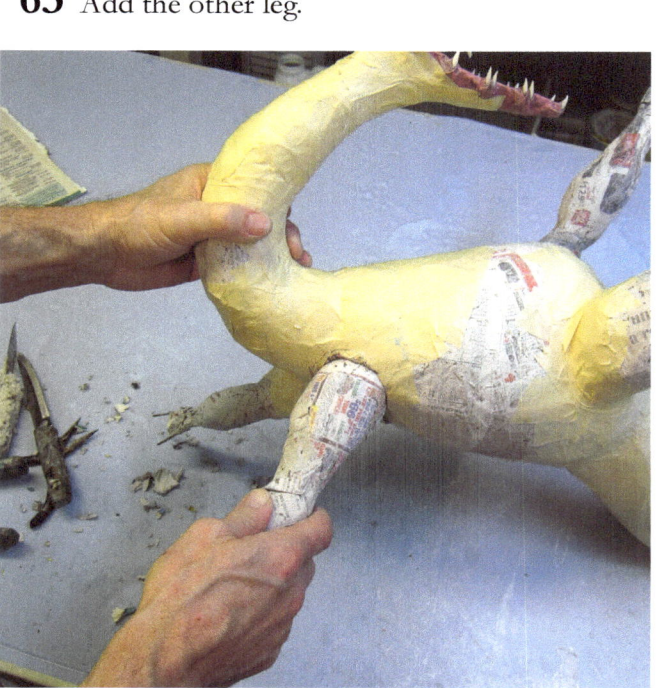

65 Even though it's early in the build it's time to take stock of the "feel" of your dragon. Moving the arms and legs even a small amount can radically alter how your dragon looks. I'll say this a number of times throughout this book - experiment as you put your dragon together. I chose this particular placement of arms and legs for a reason. I want my dragon to look like an eagle just as it snatches its prey. At the last second the wings are thrown back and the legs are thrust forward. So far this dragon fits that scenario. I like it. If this works for you, great. But it's highly likely that if you follow my advice and try a few different positions for your dragon's arms and legs, you will find an "attitude" you like better. So play around a bit......I'll wait.

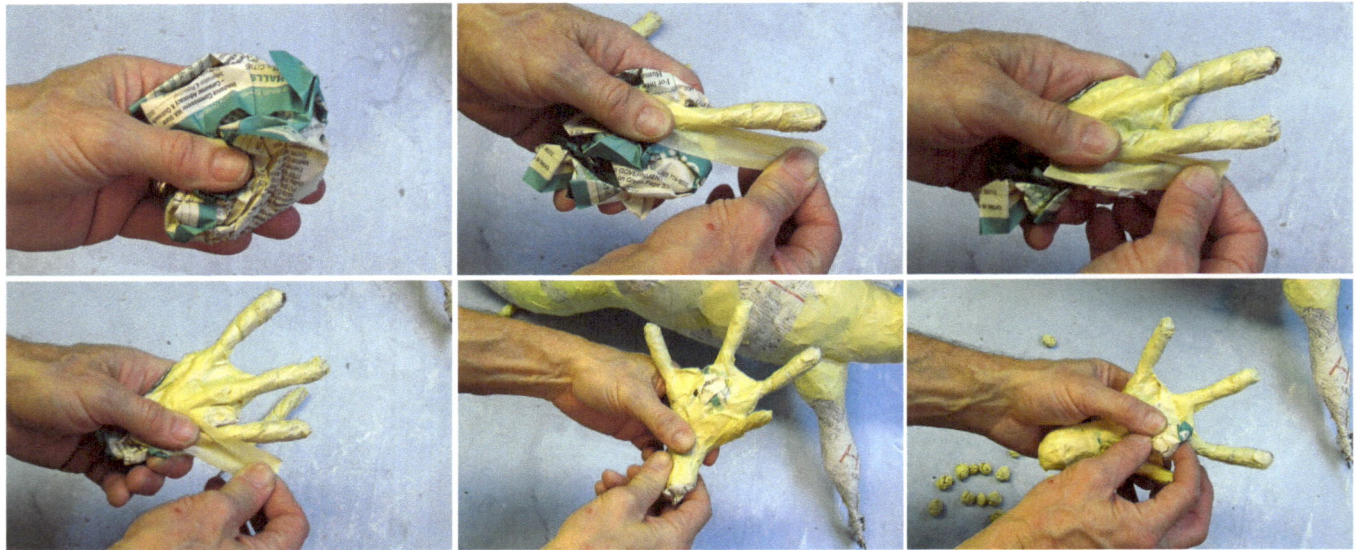

66 Now the feet. Crumple a piece of paper. Here I'm using phone book paper. I love the way it compresses. Put a toe in the middle and then wrap it with tape (in criss-cross fashion). Similarly, add other toes on each side of the first. You could stop at three toes if you want. I added a smaller, fourth toe to this foot. Use half pages of phone book (or pieces of newspaper) to crumple a few more small balls of paper. Add one to create a heel, a couple more to create pads on the bottom of the foot.

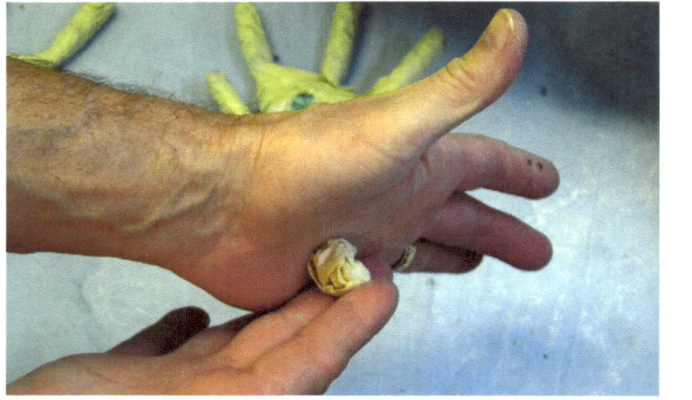
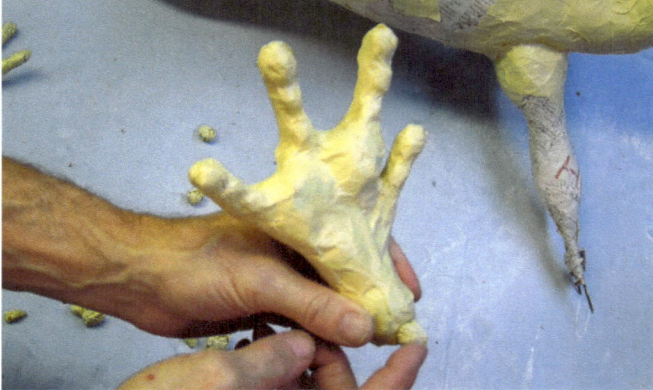

Hint: Take lengths of masking tape and roll them into a little balls. These are great for small details like knuckles. Here I used them to segment the toes. I also added one to the heel. I'll put a claw on that one.

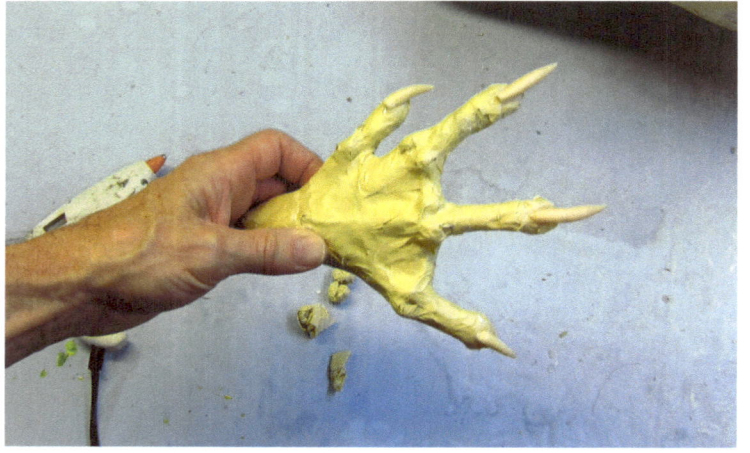

67 How much detail you add to the foot is up to you. Knuckles and other lumps and bumps are optional. I think they add a lot to the overall sophistication of the dragon. So embellish as you see fit. Finish the foot by adding claws. Just put a little hot glue on the end of the toes for these. Once you get a foot you are happy with, then make the other foot the same way.

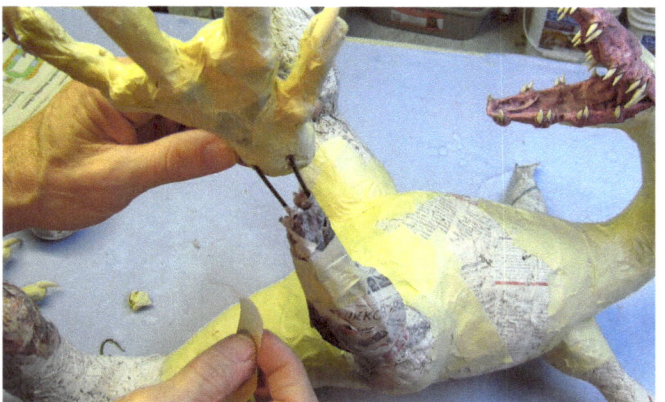 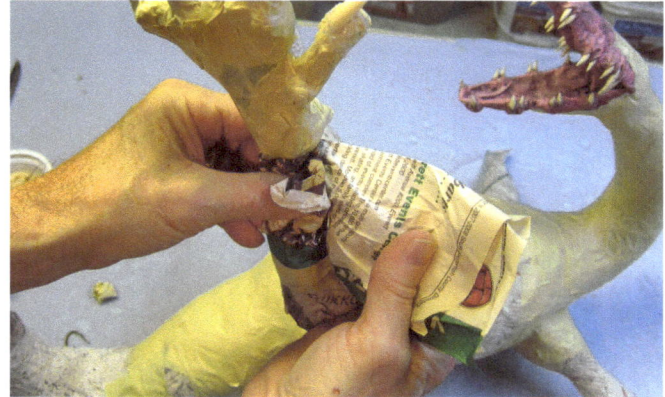

68 Attach the feet to the legs the same way you attached the upper jaw to the neck. Cut the wire loop at the end of the leg. It helps to cut the wires at an angle so they are pointed at the end. It makes it easier to pierce the tape as you push the feet onto the wires. I wanted long shins so I left gaps between the feet and the legs, then filled them in by wrapping paper around the wires and adding tape.

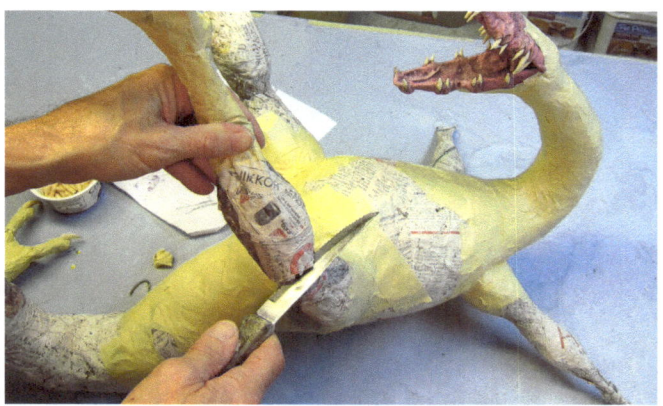 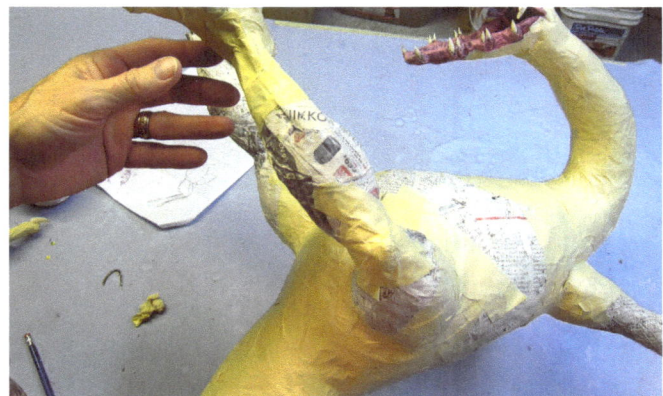

69 I decided to bend one leg slightly at the knee.   I sliced the mache with my knife.   The clothes hanger kept it in place. Of course a gap formed where I cut. I filled it with a crumpled ball of paper (which became a kneecap) and then added tape.   It goes without saying (but I'll say it anyway), you can choose to make this same change to your dragon's leg or not.   Whatever you think looks good.

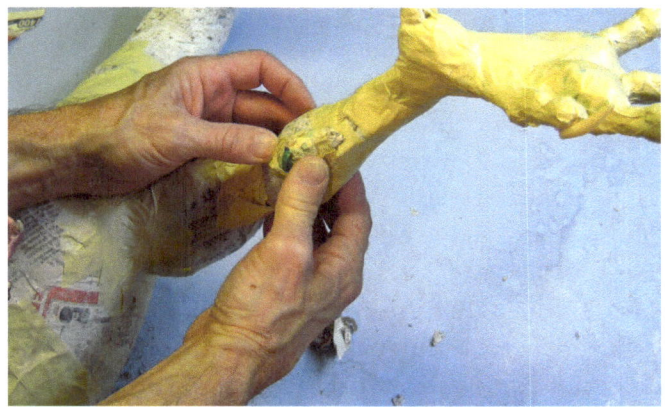 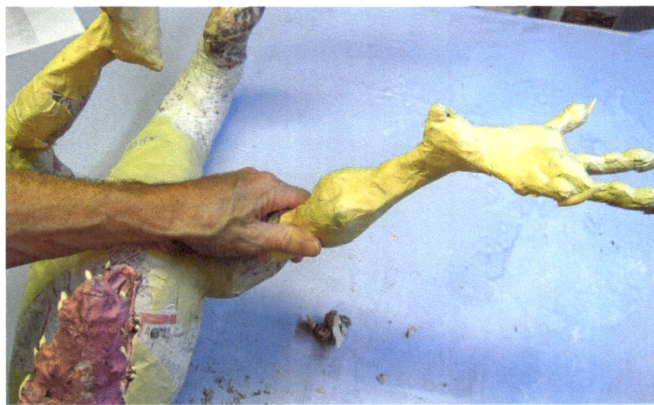

70 You might want to embellish the legs a little. I added some calves. I sliced off two small, rounded shells from my extra paper mache balls and taped them on. Of course you could also create the calves by crumpling paper and adding tape.

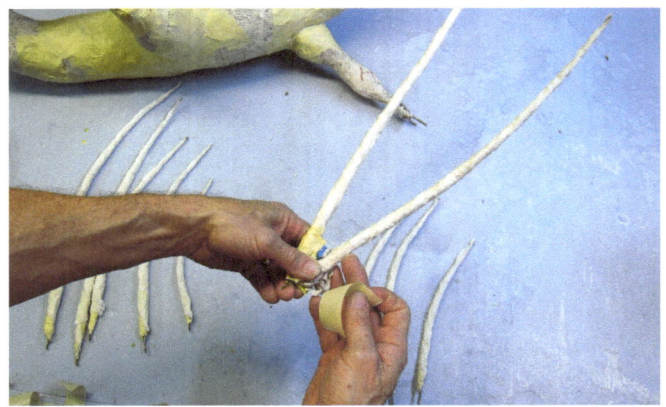 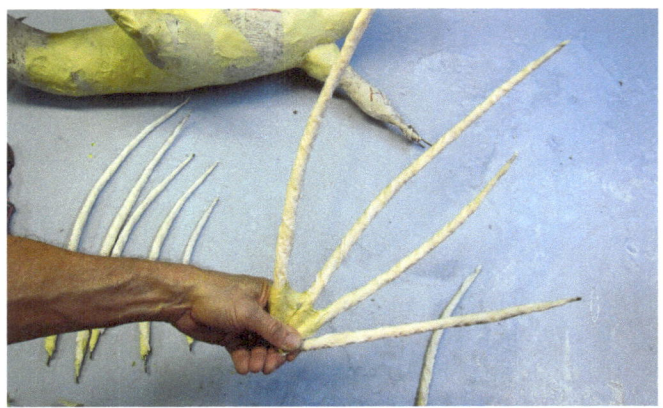

71 On to the wings. As I mentioned, these will be analogous to bat's wings. So we need to combine the long fingers into hands (of sorts). Put these together as you did the feet. Crumple a ball of paper (a little smaller than you used for the feet) and add each finger in turn using masking tape.

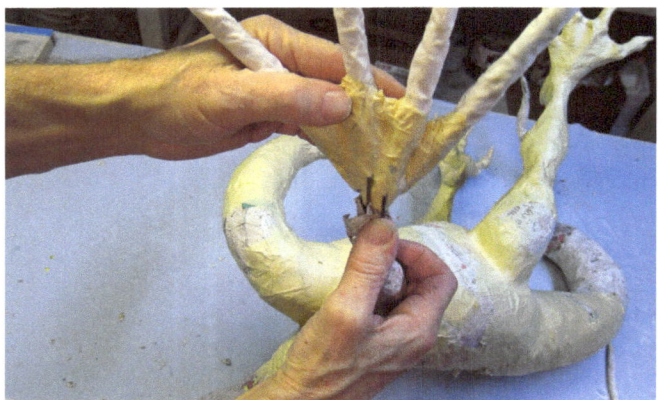 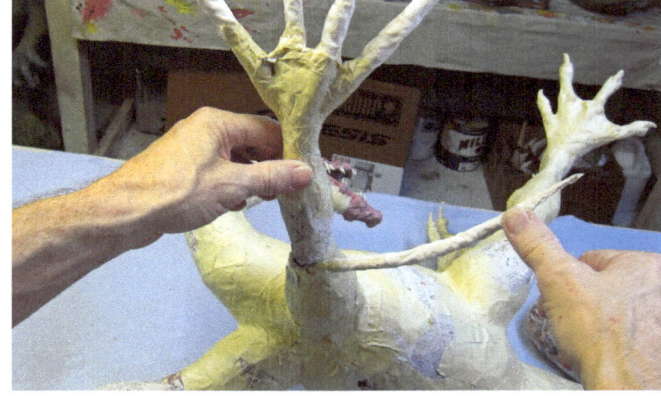

72 Once again, use the wire coming out of the arms to attach the hands. These wires add crucial strength to the wrists.

73 I like to add a "finger" at the elbow. I know, bats don't have this. To anyone who notices I say, "It's a dragon, not a bat (silly person)!"

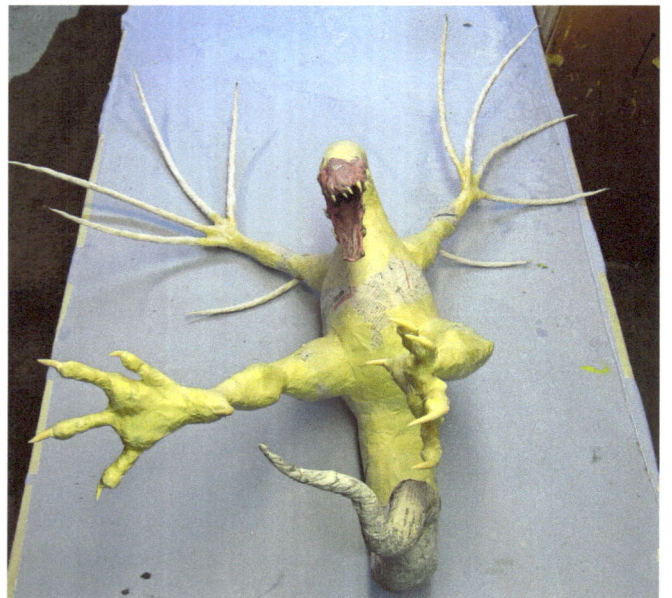

This dragon is starting to look like a dragon! At least I think so. How about you? At the risk of sounding like a broken record, you should play around a bit with your dragon. Perhaps that's not the right way to put it. You know what I mean. Bend the arms and legs. Make adjustments to the feet and toes. You can always undo your changes if you don't like them because of the hangers inside. You can make your dragon exactly like this one. But listen. Trust me on this. If you experiment with various positions you will find one that flips some deep, unconscious, psychic switch inside you and you will think, "Ahhh, this is how it's supposed to look!" Okay, I'll stop preaching about this.

VII. Cloth Mache - Part 2

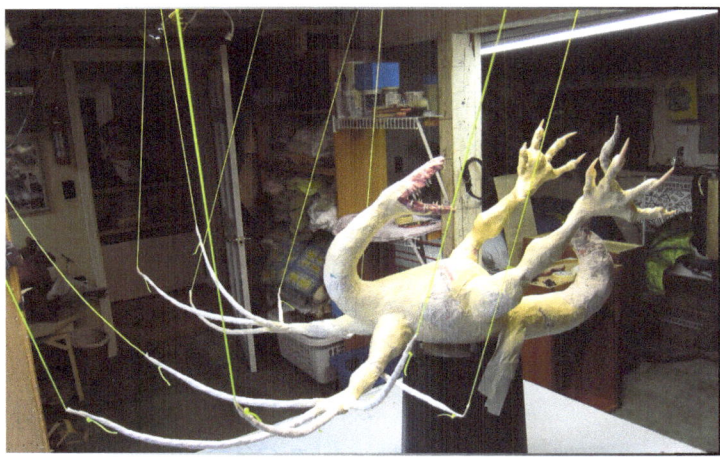

We are ready to add more of the cloth mache "skin." We'll start by making wings. A little prep work is in order.

> **You will need:**
> - **White glue**
> - **A large plastic bucket**
> - **Waste basket**
> - **Scissors**
> - **String**

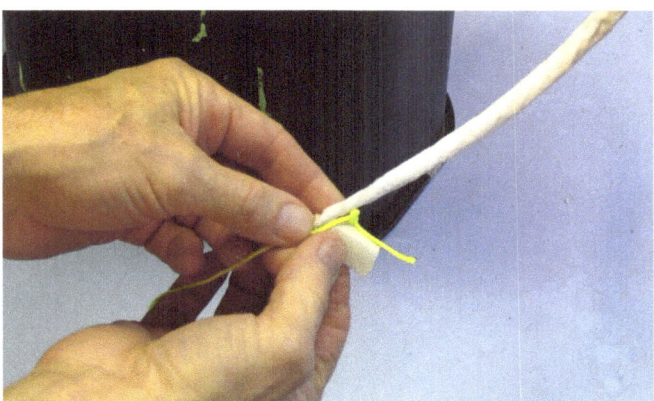 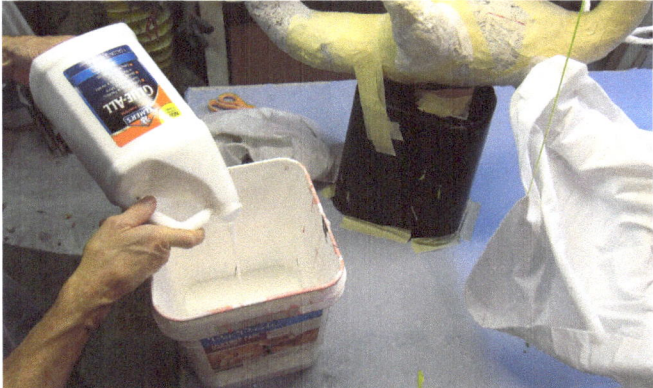

74 Lay the dragon on something like a tall waste basket. Add tape to hold it in place (see the first photo). We do this to give room for cloth to drape. Because I'll be draping large, wet, heavy pieces of cloth over the fingers, they will need support. I tape string to the end of the fingers (I tie a knot so the string doesn't slip under the tape and come off). Then I attach these strings to nails or screws in the ceiling. (Okay, so this is my studio. I realize that some of you may not want to drive screws into your ceiling. But this is important! Go ahead and do it. You can always fill the holes with Spackle.)

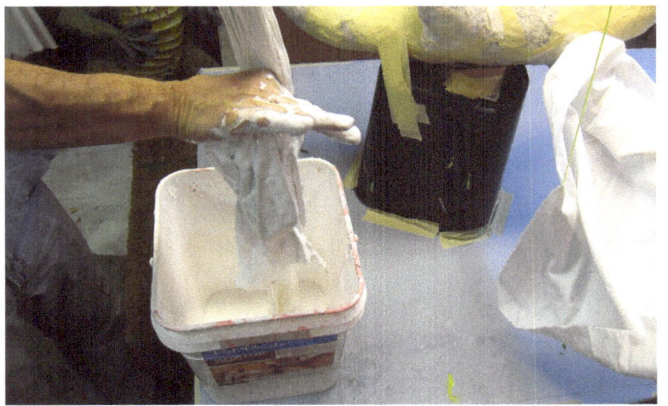 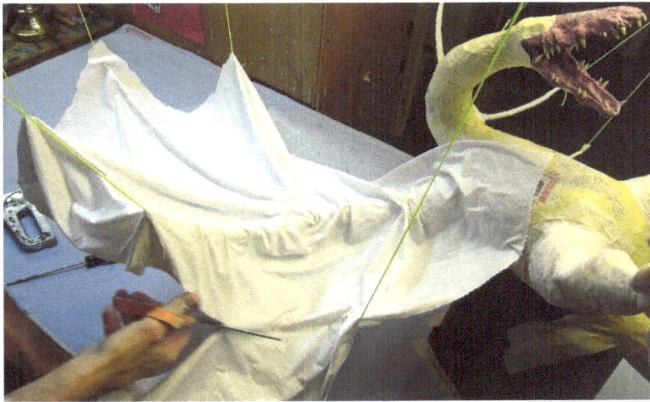

75 I use a big (kitty litter) container for this step. Soak a large piece of cloth in the glue and squeeze out the excess. Push the cloth between the fingers and onto the body of the dragon. Use scissors to cut off some of the excess cloth. These are only rough cuts. I will trim more carefully later.

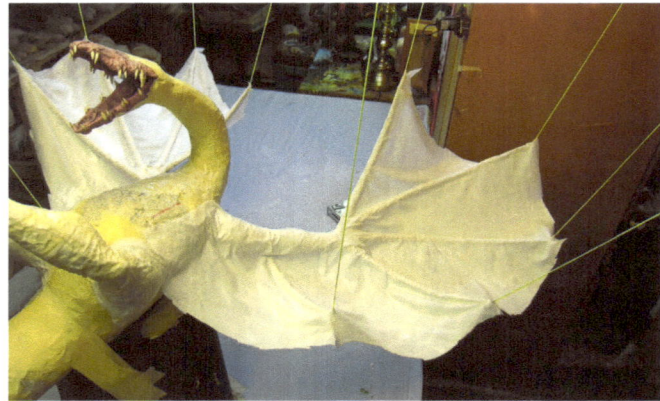

76 Manipulate the cloth until it lays evenly across the fingers. This can be challenging! I spend a long time adjusting the wet cloth. Don't get discouraged. Keep at it. Let the wings dry.

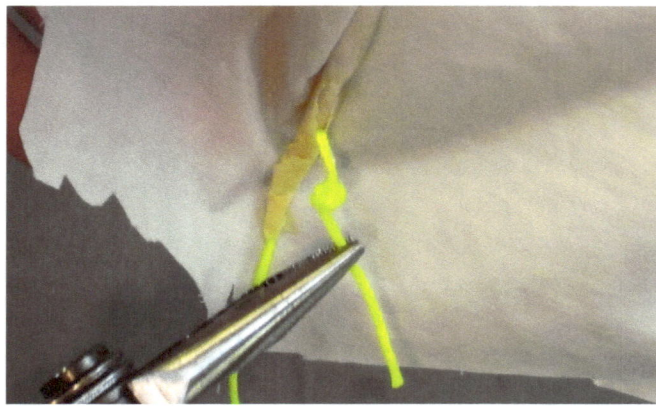

77 Once the wings are dry, turn the dragon over. Grab the strings with pliers and pull them off the fingers (they will tear through the tape).

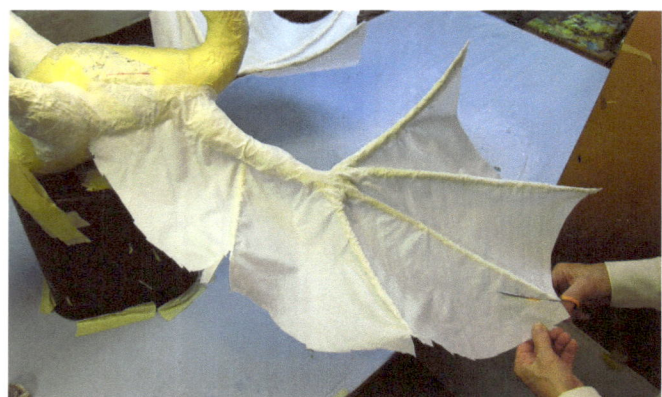

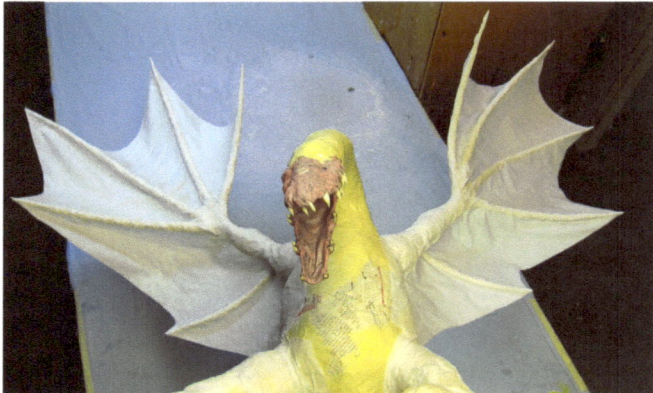

78 Once the strings are removed, turn the dragon back over. Use scissors to trim the wings. I like a scalloped look.

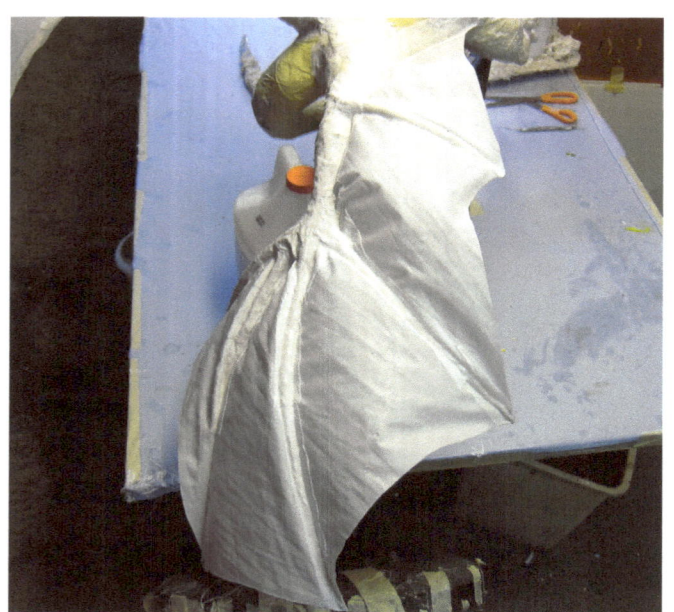

79 After trimming the wings, turn the dragon over once again. You won't drape any more cloth. But you do want to cover the fingers. Use long strips of cloth and glue for this. When these strips dry they will help lock in the general shape of the draping.

By the way... when I'm finished soaking the large pieces of cloth I pour the remaining glue back into the original container.

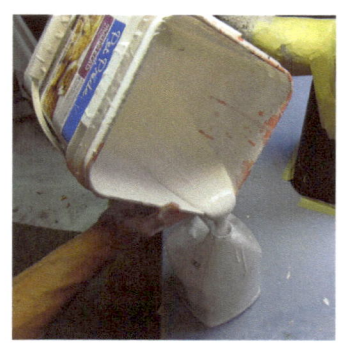

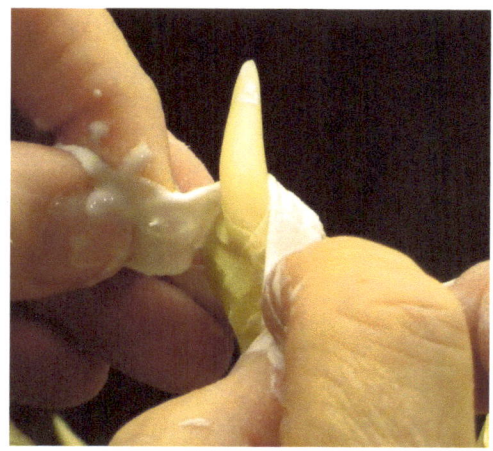
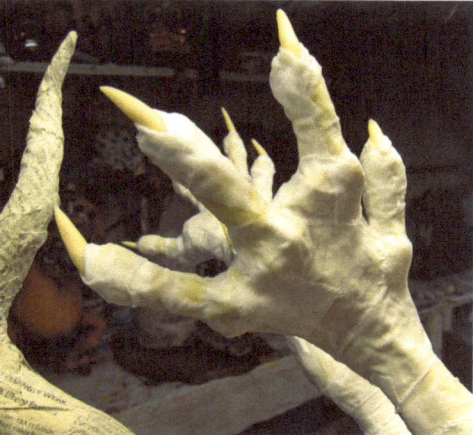

80 Now we will add cloth mache to the feet. Start by folding a small strip of glue soaked cloth and wrap it around each claw. That will give a nice definition between the claw and the toe. There are no special instructions for the rest of the foot. Just cover the rest with small pieces of cloth.

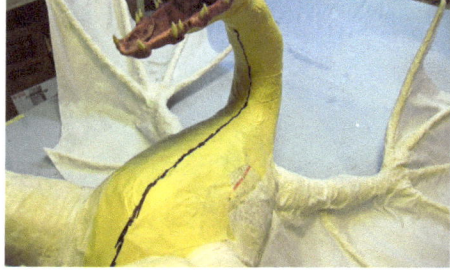
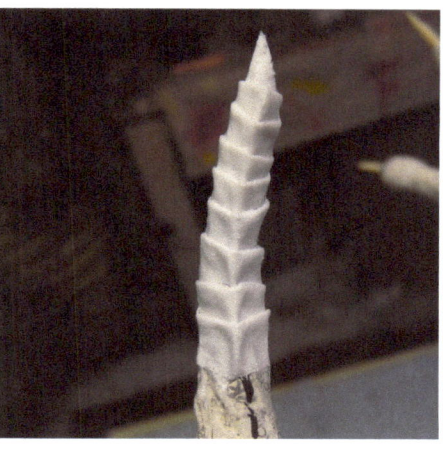
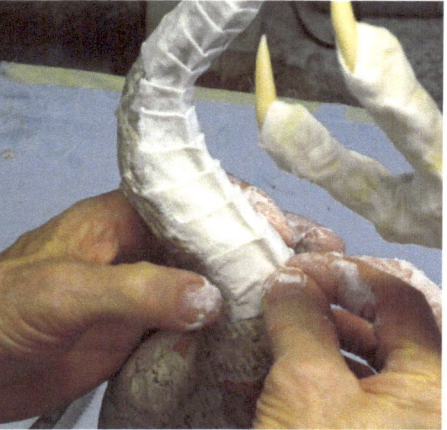

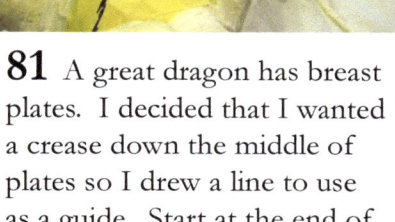

81 A great dragon has breast plates. I decided that I wanted a crease down the middle of plates so I drew a line to use as a guide. Start at the end of the tail. Apply one small strip of folded cloth over the other as you work your way up the tail. Using the line as a guide, pinch the cloth in the middle. I really like the look of the crease. Sometimes I put two or even three creases, evenly distributed, in these breastplates. Work your way along the entire length of the dragon.

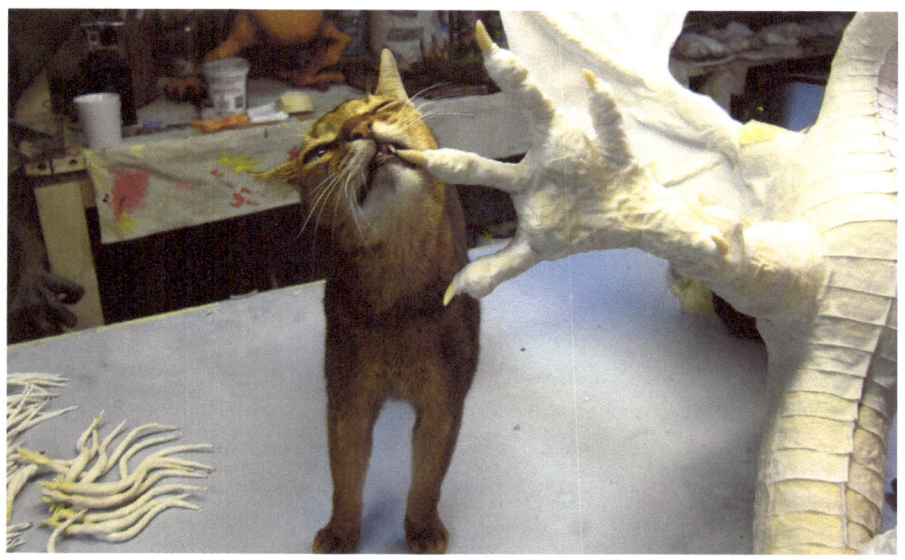

I had Eddie check my progress. I'm sure he would have given me a thumbs-up, if he had thumbs.

VIII. Final Assembly

You may have noticed that, except for adding the jaws, I haven't done any work on the dragon's head. I suppose this is another example of delayed gratification. Working on the face is my favorite part of the build. I savor the moments when the dragon begins to take on a personality. So the final sculpting involves finishing the head and then adding the all-important details.

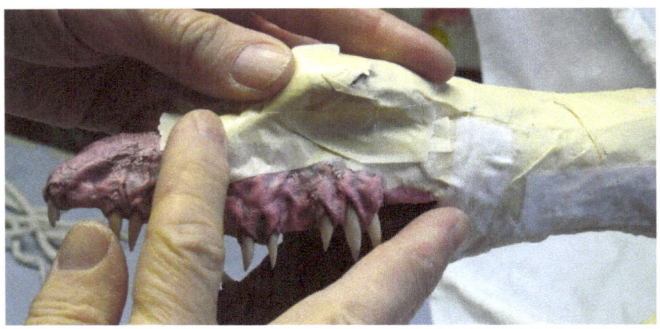 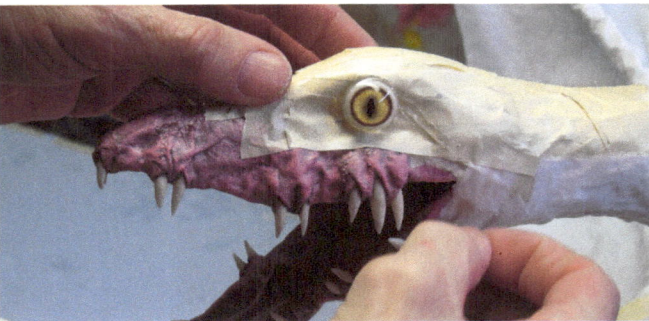

82 As you've seen, I do a lot of my sculpting with small wads of paper. Start the face by adding a forehead. Just add a wad of paper taped to the top of the head. Using a little hot glue, add the eyes. As always, experiment with the position of the eyes. Small changes will greatly alter the expression.

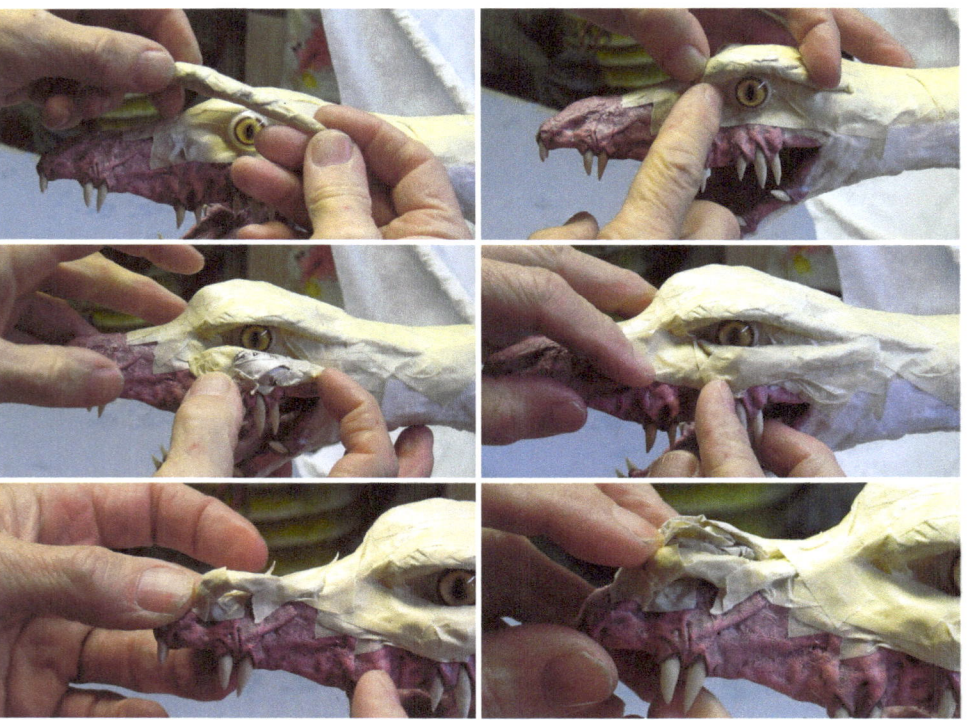

83 I decided I wanted a heavier brow. So I twisted some paper and taped it over the eyes. With another wad of paper I added some cheeks. I made a nose much like I made the eyebrows. I created nostrils with a little bridge of twisted paper. It might have been easier to just add a round shell from my extra paper mache balls and then punch holes for nostrils. Enjoy this part. Take your time. Work until you get a face you love.

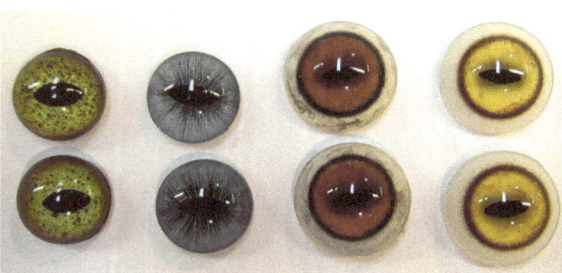

A quick note about eyes. I love glass eyes. As I mentioned in the supply list, I like taxidermy eyes. There are many choices. It's an important decision. Spend some time looking online for just the right eyes. You can even buy "blanks" and make your own customized eyes. I used the eyes on the far right They are 16 mm in diameter.

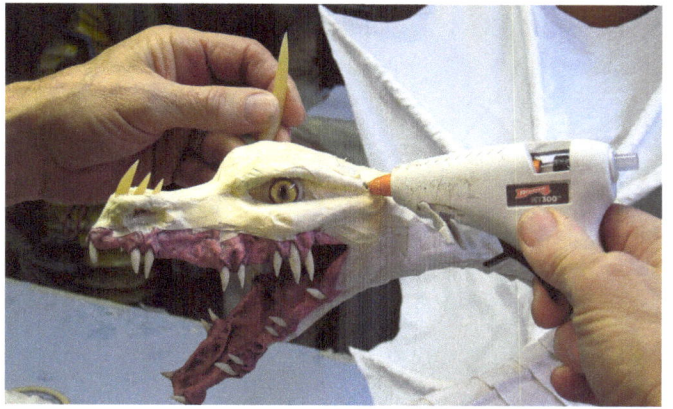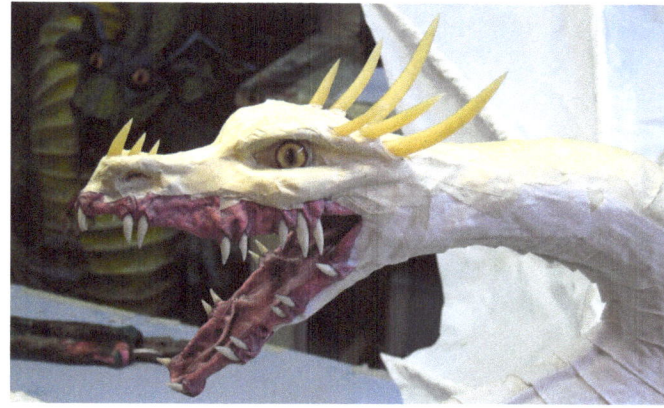

84 Dragons need horns. So add a few, or many. I hot glued a few small ones on the nose. Then I added some long ones behind the eyes. I wanted ears on this dragon. People have told me that dragons are reptilian and don't have ears. But I want my dragon to come to me when I call. So he needs ears.

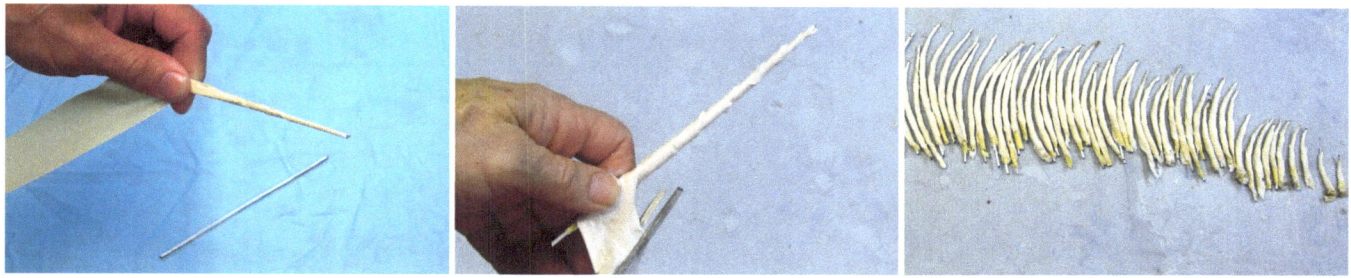

85 These ears will look like tiny wings. So I make them the same way (see the photos below). I also want spines running down the entire length of the back. These are just little "fingers" like I made for the wings earlier, except they are smaller. As before, I used pieces of clothes hanger, but this time I didn't twist any paper around them. I just wrapped the wire with masking tape and then with cloth and glue. I made a lot of these spines in various lengths because I wasn't sure how many I would need. I curved them slightly. (They just look better that way.) I used the first eight of these spines for the ears.

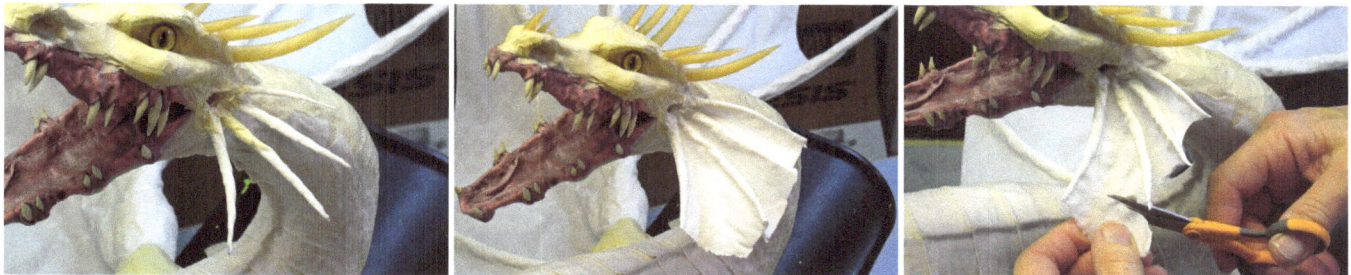

86 Poke holes in the side of the head with something sharp (like an ice pick). Squirt a little hot glue into these holes and then stick in the spines. Cut a hole in the side of the head for the ear canal. Drape this with cloth and let dry. I added scallops just like I did with the wings. These are pretty elaborate ears. I like the look. But you know, just a couple holes on the sides of the head would suffice for dragon ears.

At this point I decided that I also wanted to add a few "whiskers" (for lack of a better term) to this face. Since the face of this dragon is fairly small, these whiskers needed to be even thinner than the spines I'm using on the back. I realize that I've gotten a bit obsessive with this face. If you like your dragon face the way it is, then skip this next step.

I used smaller gauge wire for these whiskers. You can find small gauge wire at any hobby supply store. I'm using "Stem Wire" (18 gauge). To keep these really thin I just wrapped them with cloth and glue strips (no paper or tape). This is a little tricky. Cut the strip of cloth at an angle. Pinch the wire and cloth together and turn the finger. The cloth will wrap itself around the wire as you turn.

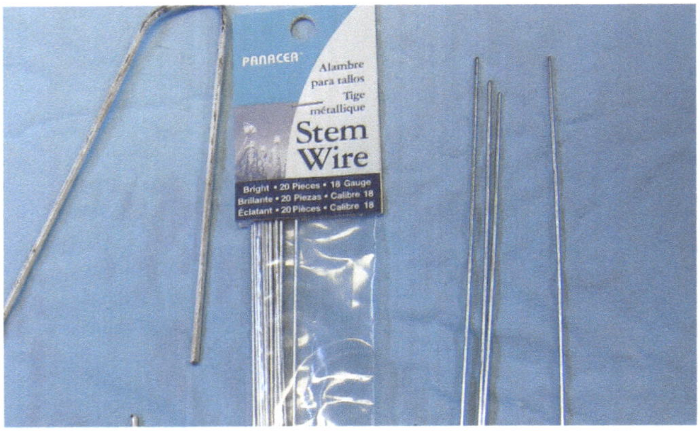

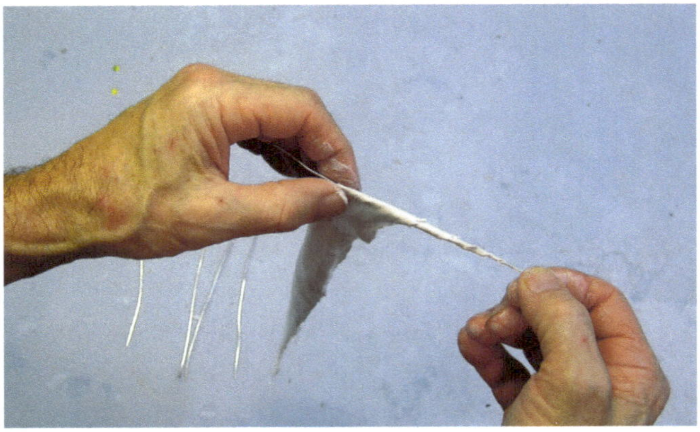

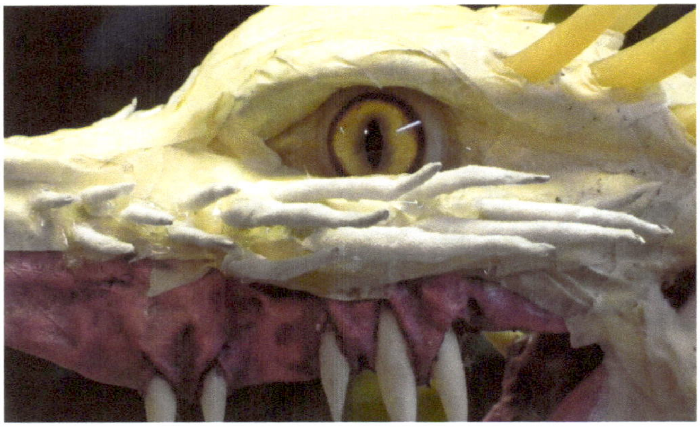

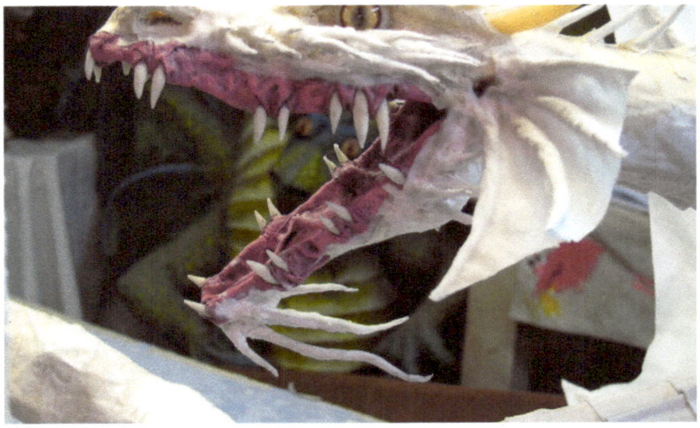

87 I made these whiskers all the same size. Then, after they were dry I cut them into the various lengths I wanted. I put a few of these whiskers on the cheek and also on the chin and jowls.

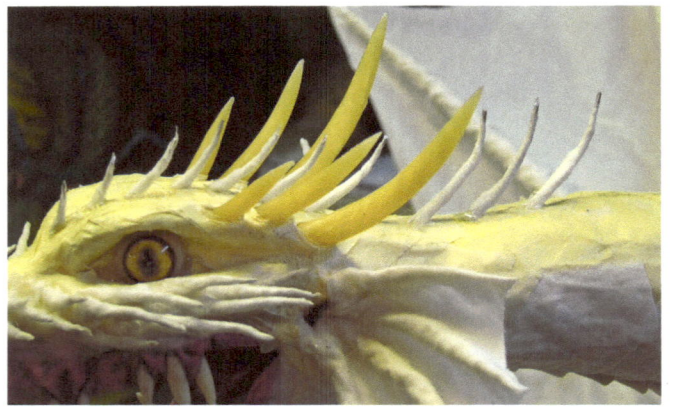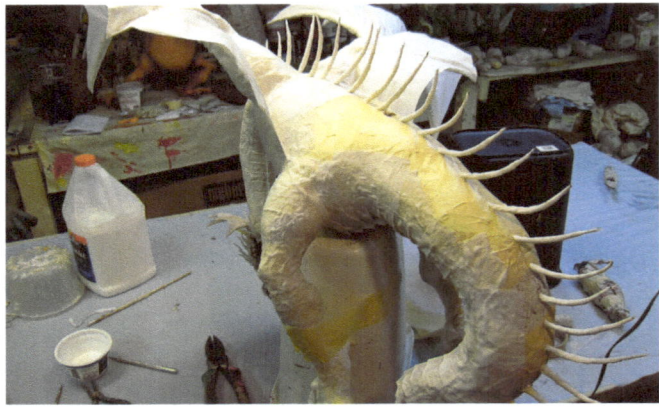

88 I used some of these smaller whiskers on the top of the head to begin the row of spines. When I got to the neck, I started using the thicker spines I made earlier. I poked regularly spaced holes along the entire dragon. I pushed the spines into the holes after squirting in a little hot glue. This looks great. For an even more dramatic effect, add cloth between the spines. Then cut some scallops with scissors. You can see examples of this on some of the dragons in this book (see the neck on the trophy on page 39).

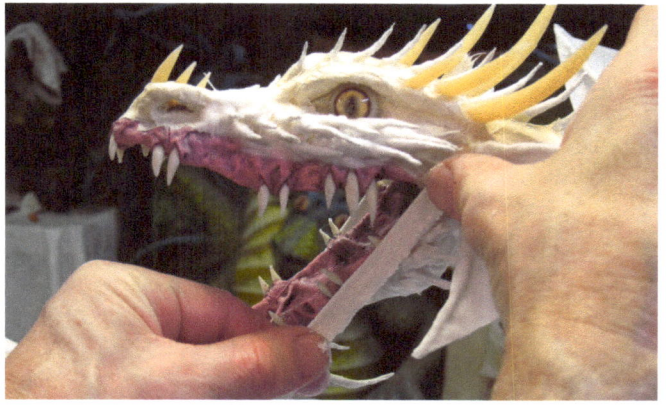
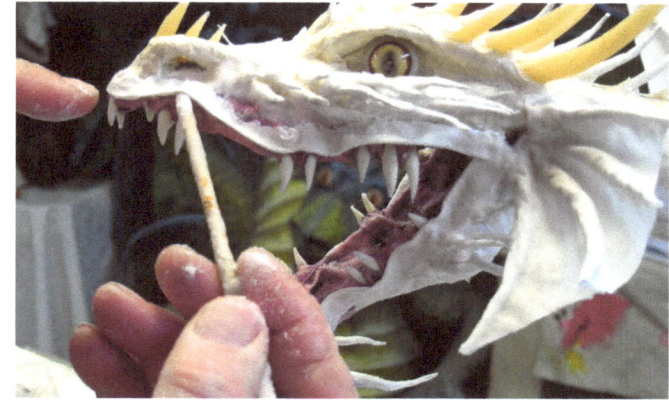

89 Finish adding cloth mache to the face and the rest of the dragon. Lips first. Use a strip of cloth long enough to go around the lower jaw. Fold it in half to make a lip. Fold it twice to make Angelina Jolie lips. Starting at the ear, wrap it around the jaw. Add the upper lip the same way. Add a few wrinkles and dimples in the cloth to make the mouth more interesting.

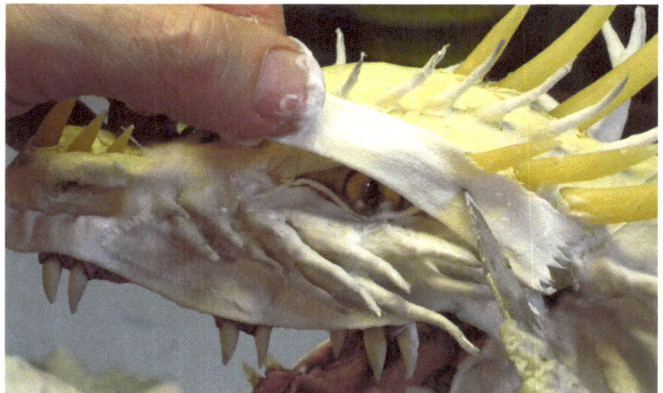
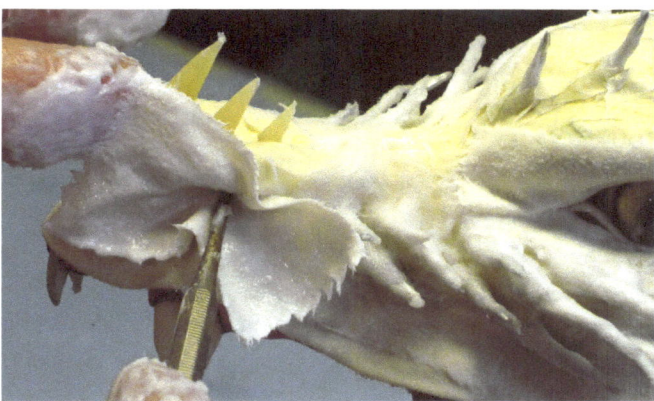

90 Fold two more pieces of cloth. Put one under the eye for a lower lid, and one over the eye for an upper lid.

91 Push a piece of cloth into the nose hole. Then fold the cloth over on the outside to create a nostril.

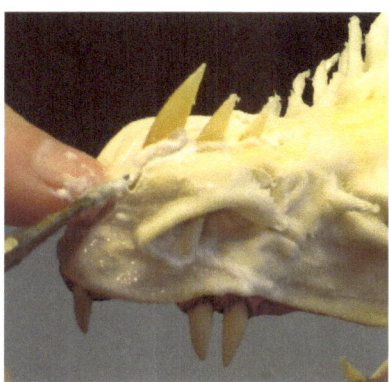
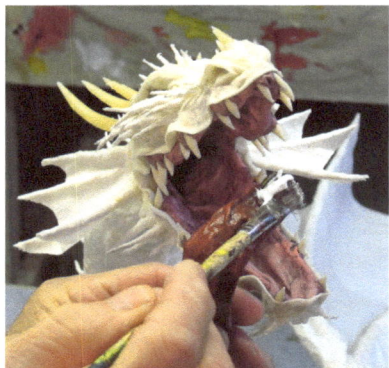
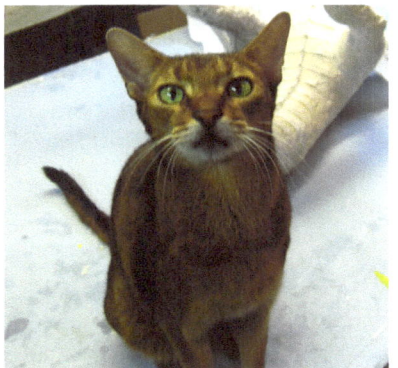

92 I like to wrap the base of each horn with a little strip of folded cloth. Finish the head by covering any bare spots with small pieces of cloth.

93 Add the tongue. Use hot glue, or paint glue on the base, and then push it into the throat.

94 Feed the "assistant."

Last, but not least.... scales.   Scales are completely optional. They are a lot of work. But this kind of detail is really worth the effort. There are several kinds of scales you can use. I'll show you my favorite here.   I'll show you another option in the Trophy section of the book.

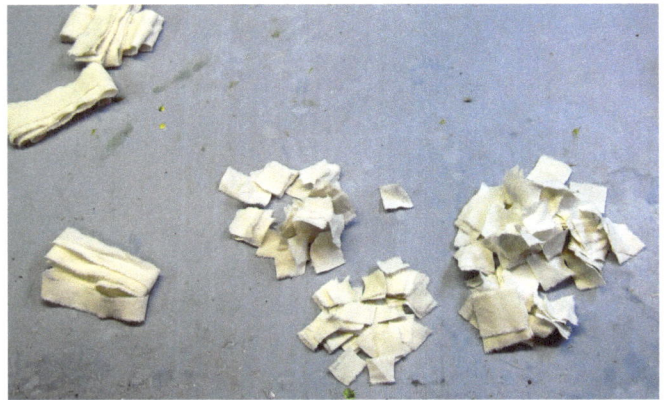

95 Tear some thin strips of cloth (about ¾ inch wide). Then cut the strips into squares. If you want larger scales then make bigger squares by tearing wider strips of cloth.

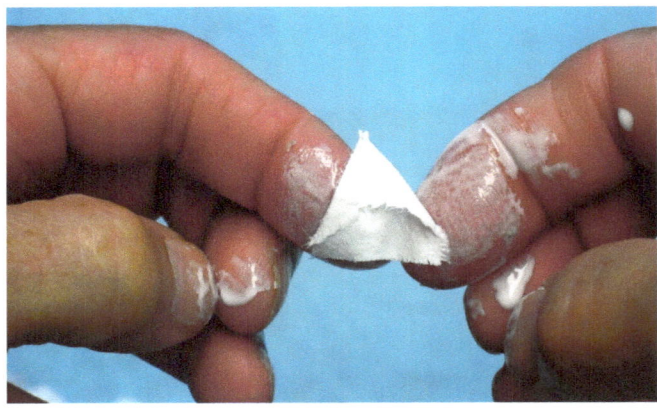

96 Dip a square in glue and then fold the corners together to make a triangle. I will use various sized scales on different parts of the dragon.

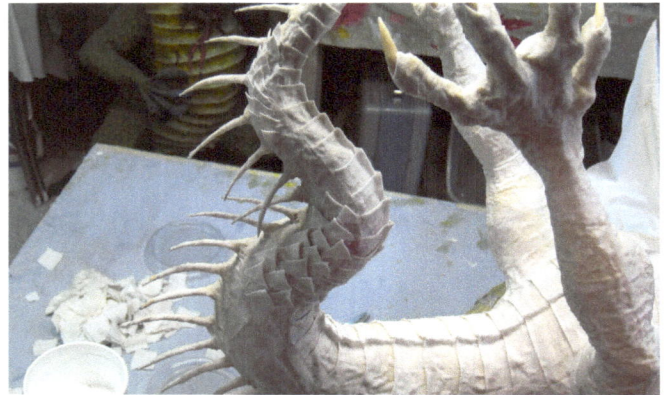

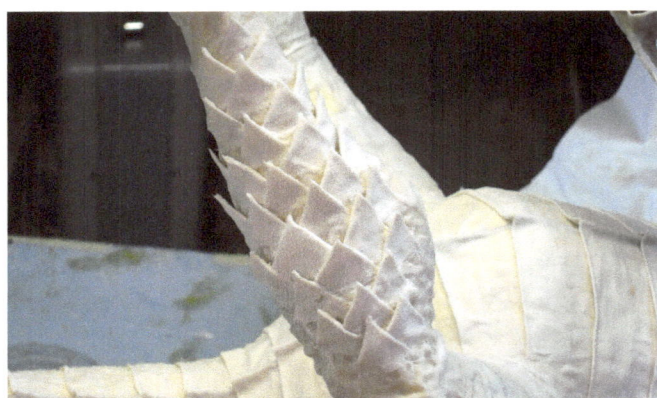

97 Apply scales like a bricklayer applies bricks. Start with one. Then straddle that scale with two others. Add successive rows by placing new scales between the previous ones. Start low on the tail or the leg and work your way up the dragon.

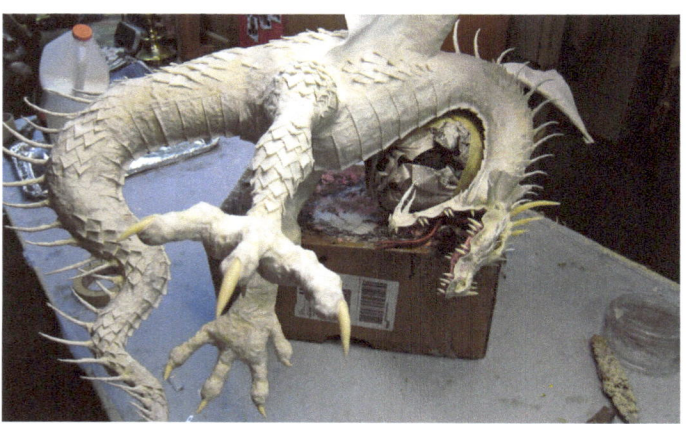

If you are really ambitious you can add scales over the entire dragon. I've done this many times. But here is another important hint. Your dragon will look just as good with well placed patches of scales as it would by completely covering the dragon. This is especially true once the dragon is painted.   Look at photos of my dragons. You will see what I mean.

IX. Painting

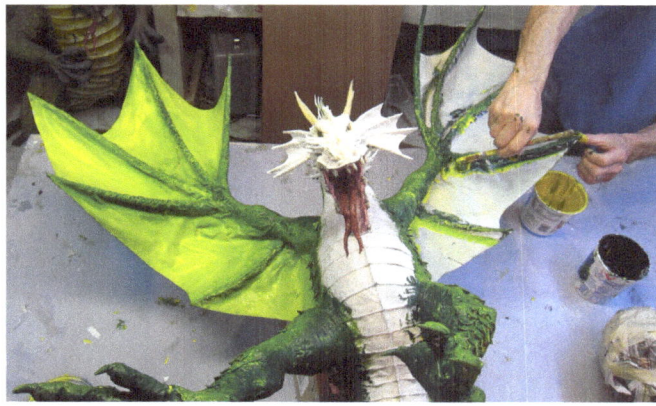

What you need:
- **All-purpose paints**
- **Brushes**
- **Courage**

I paint in threes stages. The base coat comes first. Then I accentuate the details by "blackwashing." Finally I add highlights. More about each of these stages in a minute. First, some advice about colors. Don't buy orange or green paint. Leave your options open. Buy only primary colors, red, blue, and yellow, along with black and white. Then you will have all possible colors at your disposal.

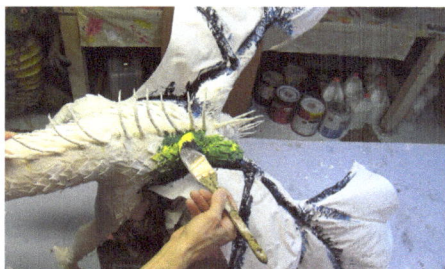
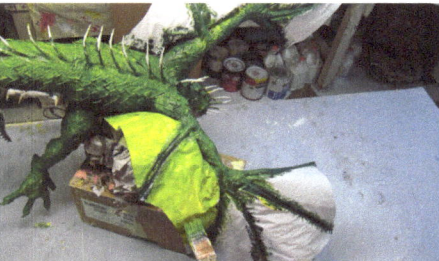
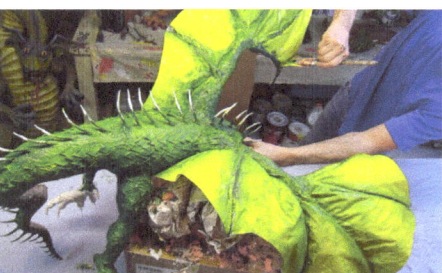

98 Because I want a greenish dragon, I will use only blue and yellow paint for the base coat. If you choose a different color scheme, consider using two colors, one dark and one light (relative to each other). Red and yellow for example. Well, anything and yellow I suppose. Paint blue (dark) under the arms and the over the fingers. While this is still wet, stick your brush in the yellow (the light color) and paint the other surfaces. Blend the two colors where they meet. Generally speaking, blend as you go but not so much that you lose the variation in color. You do not want a monotone paint job.

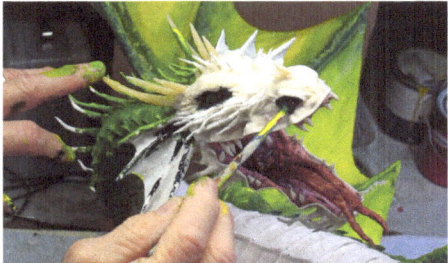
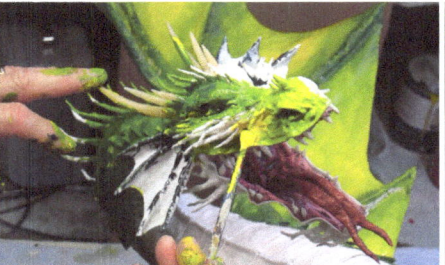
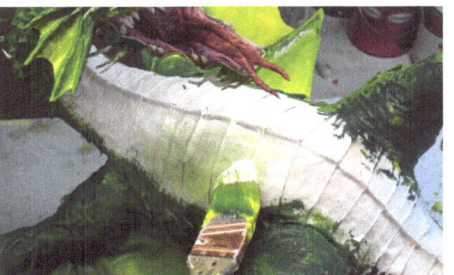

99 Work your way around the dragon. Blue in the eye sockets and the nostrils and then yellow for the rest of the face. Blue on the undersides of the legs, the calves and the soles of the feet, then yellow on the top, the shins, thighs, and tops of the feet. I like a more pastel underbelly. So I add some white paint when I get to the breastplates. I paint this base coat in one sitting. I call my method, "fast and furious." It helps to have a few cups of coffee. Don't worry if you get paint all over your hands. It washes off. For you nervous types, remember that you can always fix painting mistakes with more paint once everything is dry. Remember, don't worry about getting paint on the teeth, horns, and claws. It is easily scraped off once the paint has dried.

I know what you are thinking. "My dragon is beautiful!" Now I'm going to tell you to ruin it. Well, that's what you will think. But that won't happen! Blackwashing will make your dragon even more beautiful. It will accentuate the details you worked so hard to make. My favorite crazy artist, Bill Alexander, used to say, "You can't have the light without the dark!" That seems to apply here (although he may have meant something completely different). I'll save you the shock. On the left is the very pretty, pre-blackwashed dragon. On the right, the dirty looking, post-blackwashing. Everything will be fine.

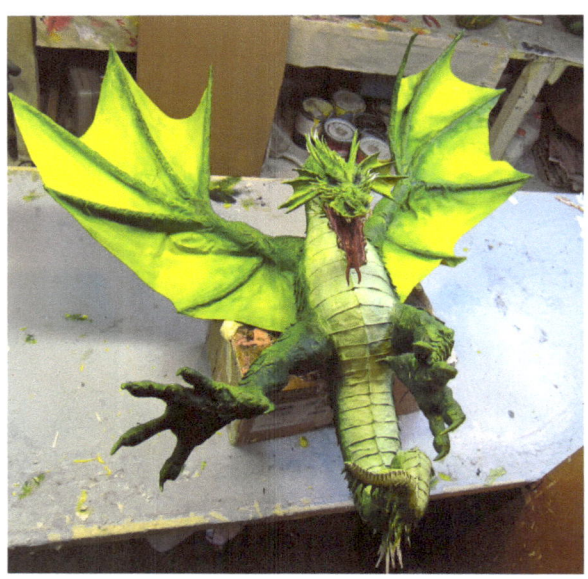
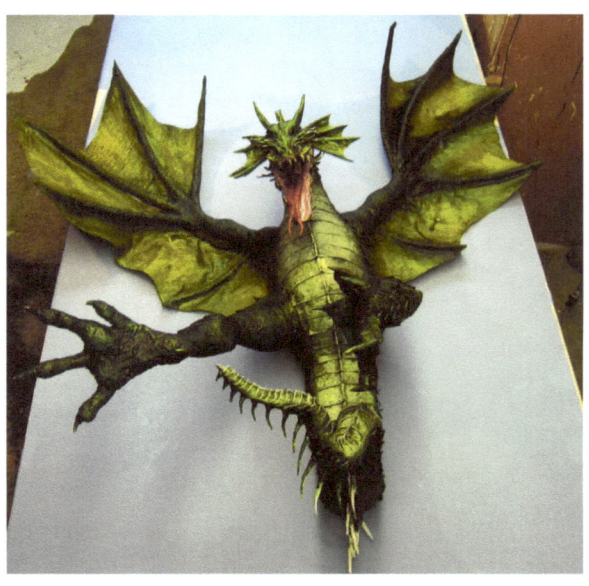

100 Be brave. Blackwash your dragon. Just add some water to black paint. How much water you add will determine how dark the black accents will be. Paint a section and then wipe it off with a slightly

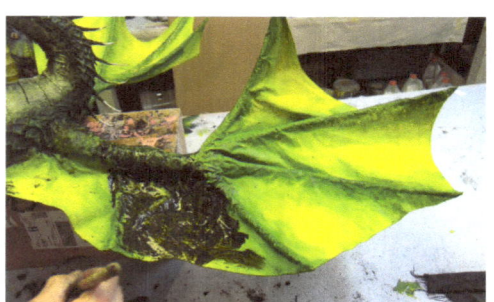
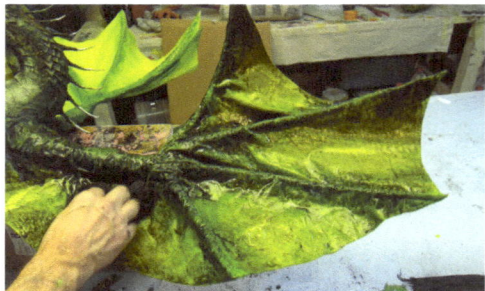

damp rag before it dries. Section by section blackwash the entire dragon. Don't worry if the paint dries too quickly and gets too dark. After the black is dry...

101 ...add back some highlights. With a little paint on your brush touch up the wings, the belly...

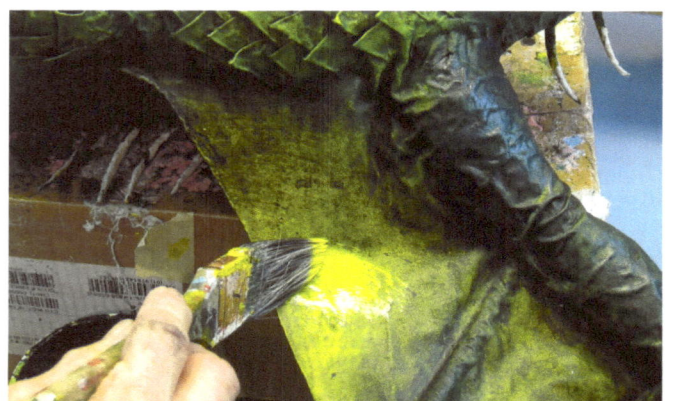
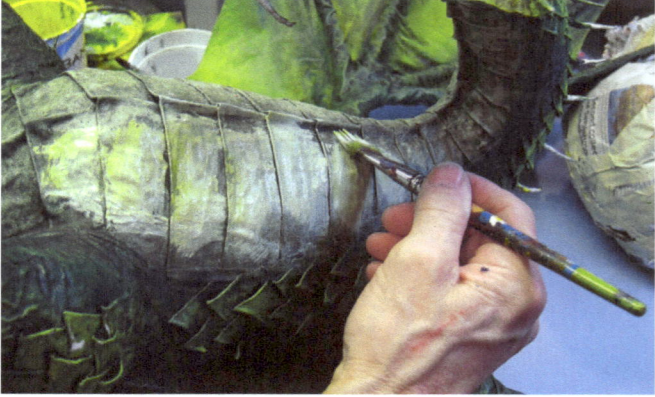

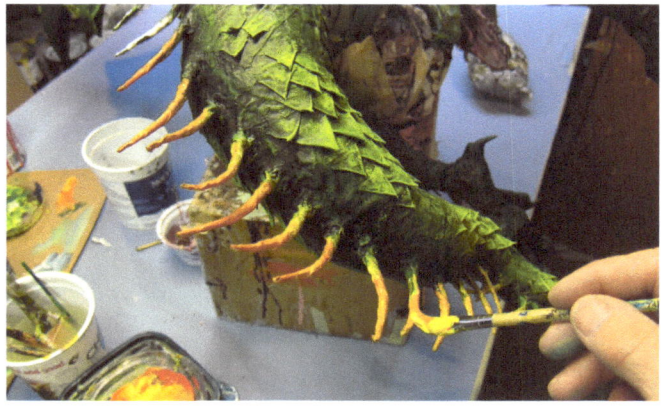

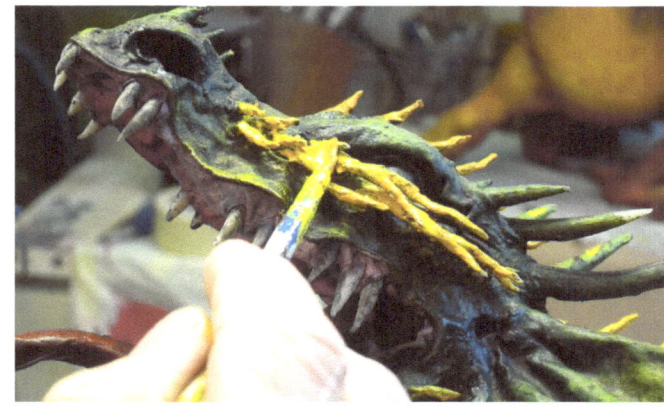

102 ... and the scales. Just run your brush over the high spots. After adding highlights paint the spines and whiskers. Once again, it looks like I'm using orange paint. But I'm not. I started with a little red paint on my brush and then added yellow while it was still wet. It resulted in a nice gradation from orange to yellow.

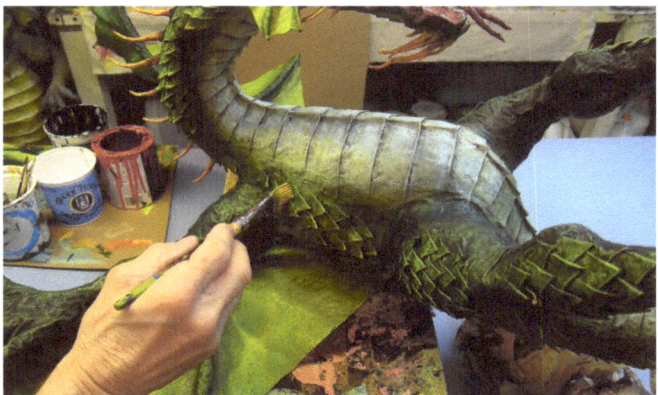

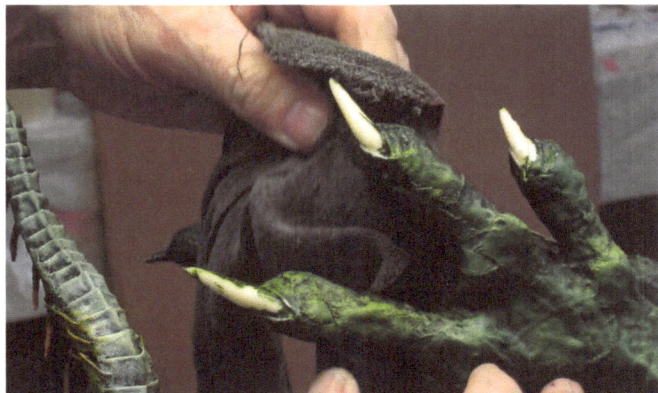

103 While I had a little orange paint on my brush, I ran it lightly over the patches of scales just to add a little more color variation.

104 Finally, remove the paint that got on the polymer clay claws and teeth. Brush on a little water to loosen the paint. Then you can wipe most of it off with a damp rag.

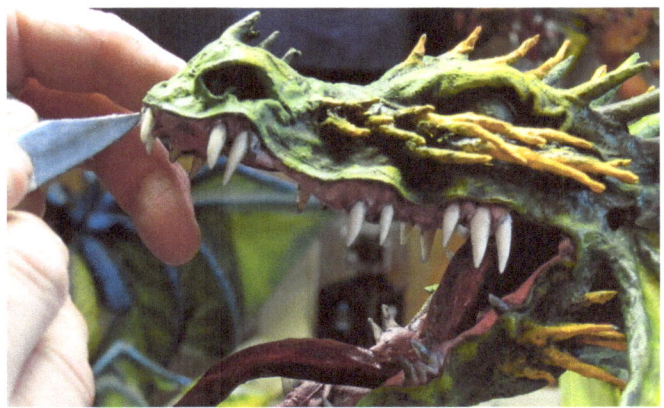

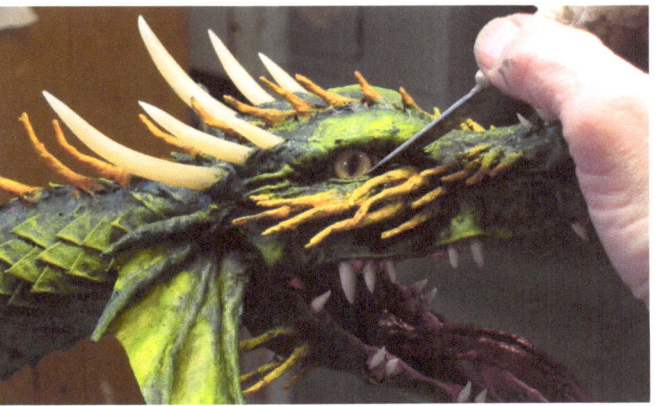

105 Use the tip of a knife to scrape the more stubborn paint that won't come off with the rag.

106 Scrape the paint off the eyes. No matter how many times I do this, it gives me a thrill. The dragon comes alive!

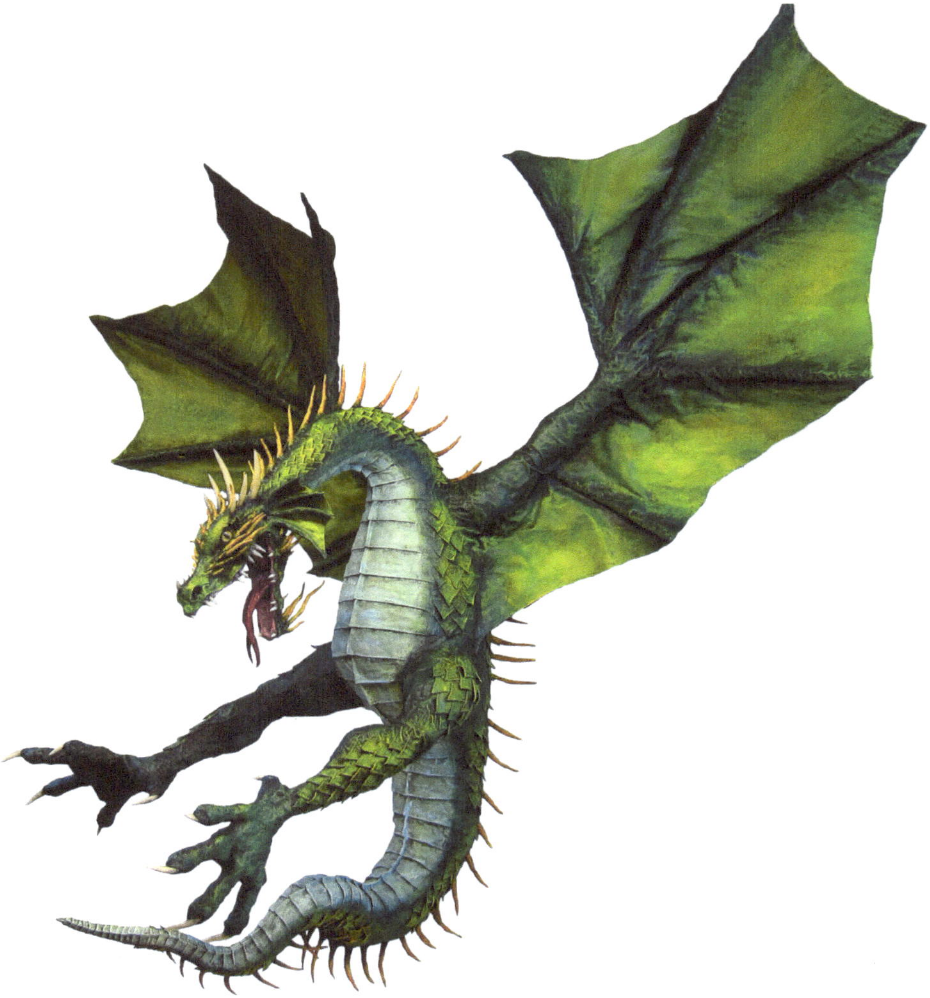

Finished!

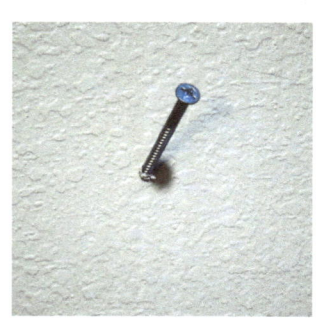

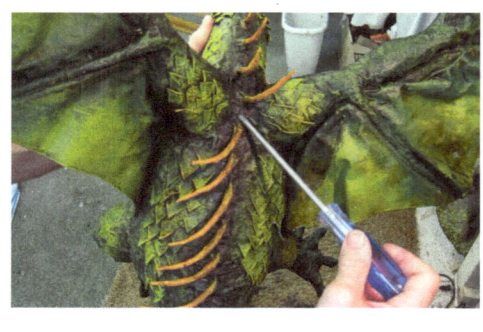

Well, almost finished. If you made a dragon like mine, you will need to hang it. I hang these kinds of dragons (and trophies) on one long screw (2 ½ or 3 inches) driven into the wall. To insure that it will hold the weight, drive it in at an angle, pointed slightly upward. Also make sure you hit a stud with the screw. Drywall alone is usually not strong enough to hold this kind of weight. I punch a hole into the back of the dragon for the screw in the wall. To hang the dragon I push it onto the screw. Note in the photo on the right that I bent over the spines on the back so that the dragon could be more flush against the wall. If your dragon is large or particularly heavy, then you might need to add a couple more layers of cloth mache around the hole to reinforce that area.

Of course you can make dragons that sit or stand. Sitting is no problem. But if you want your dragon to stand, then use the tail as a third leg. (Look at the last page in the book.) Congratulations!

X. Trophies

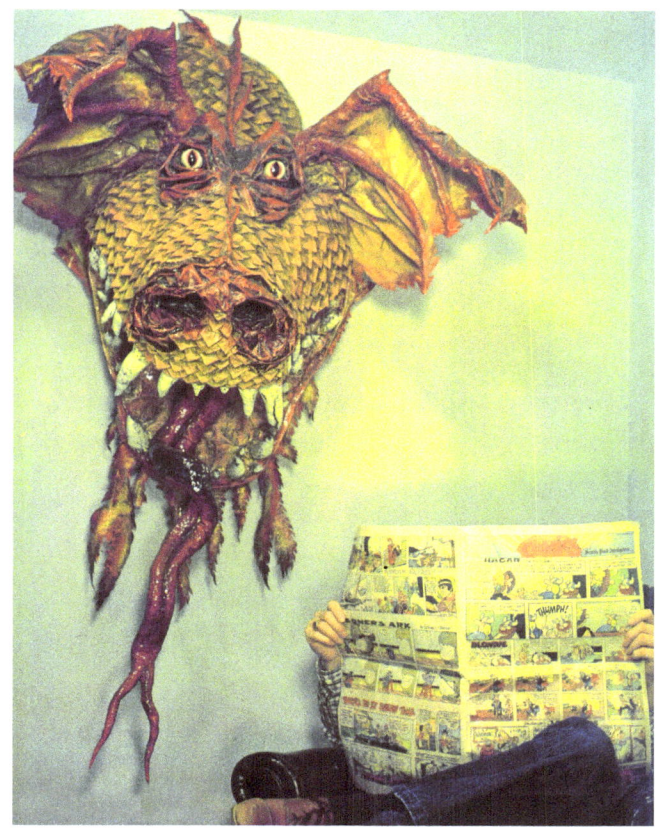

There will come a time when you want to make a big dragon. Maybe even a "full size" dragon (which could be any size I suppose, so long as it's sort of large). But it's not practical to make a 20 foot long dragon. Or maybe you are a busy person and you just don't have time to make a full dragon. Maybe you like the idea of hanging some sort of animal trophy on your wall, but not the notion of actually killing the animal. Or maybe you just want a dragon's head over the baby's crib to ward off evil spirits. A nice dragon trophy is perfect for all of these situations. All of the ferociousness, none of the toes.

I make two kinds of trophies. Some just hang on the wall (like the one on the left, which by the way is the first trophy I ever made). I'll show you how to make those first. For lack of a better term I'll just call them "simple" trophies. Others are mounted on some sort of plaque. I'll show you how to make those too. I don't want to be too redundant however. So I'll show you how to "engineer" the trophies but not spend too much time on the things I've already shown you. After all, sculpting a big dragon face is pretty much the same as sculpting a small one. No matter which kind of trophy you make, it all starts with jaws. Make those first, along with a tongue, just like I showed you earlier in the book except

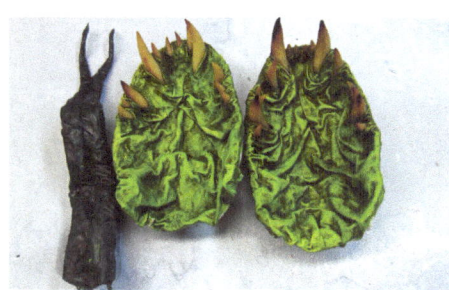

that you will want to make them larger. The photos here show various sized jaws I have used for trophies. The jaws on the immediate left are about 12 inches long. The pink ones are 14 inches, and the green ones below are 30 inches long.

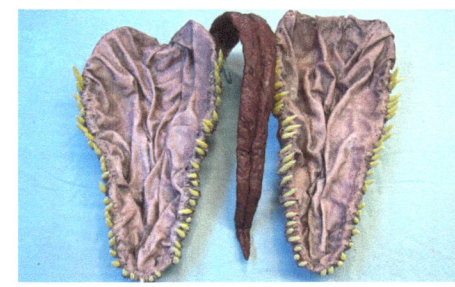

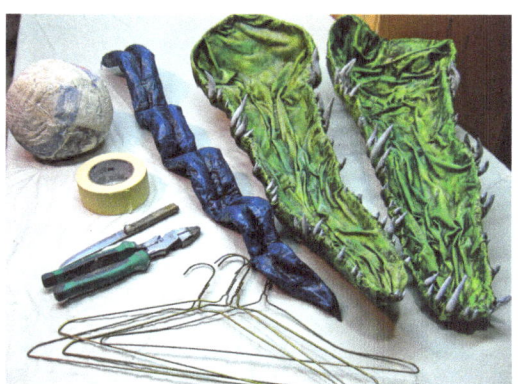

For a Simple Trophy you will need:
- **Pre-made jaws and tongue**
- **A few clothes hangers**
- **Your knife and pliers**
- **Masking tape**
- **An extra paper mache ball or two**

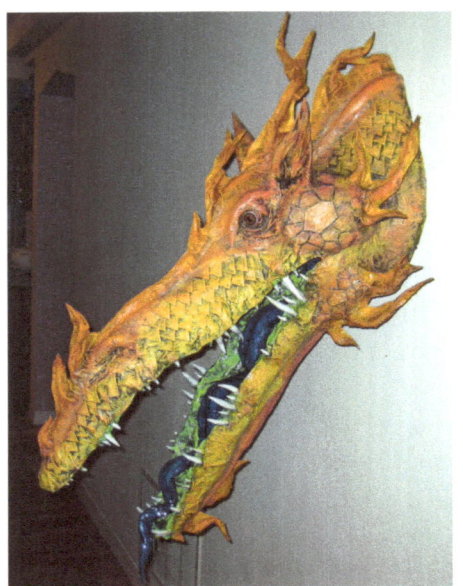

The hard part about making a trophy is not the sculpting. It is the engineering. By that I mean you must consider the forces at work when building something large and potentially heavy. You don't want to build your beautiful dragon only to watch it tear itself off the wall! As a rule of thumb, the further the trophy sticks out from the wall, the greater the force will be (the "torque") acting upon that little screw in the wall holding it up. So if you have a long jaw and/or a long neck you will need more reinforcement in various places. How do you do that? With wire clothes hangers, of course! And maybe a little thicker paper or cloth mache in spots. More about that later.

I can't show you the specifics of every possible size and shape of trophy. I'm hoping that you'll choose a reasonably sized trophy for your first, and that you will be able to extend these ideas later when you make that giant trophy to put over the garage.

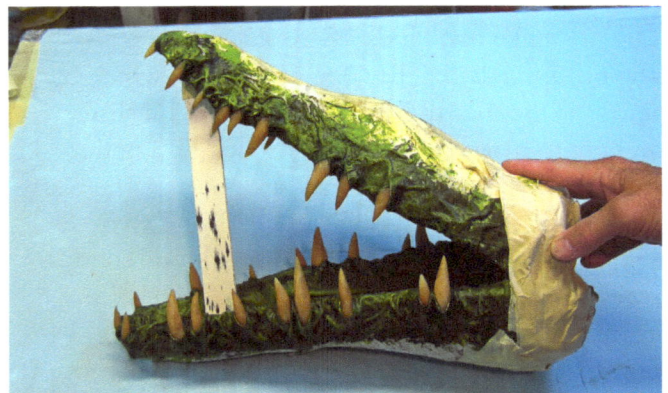
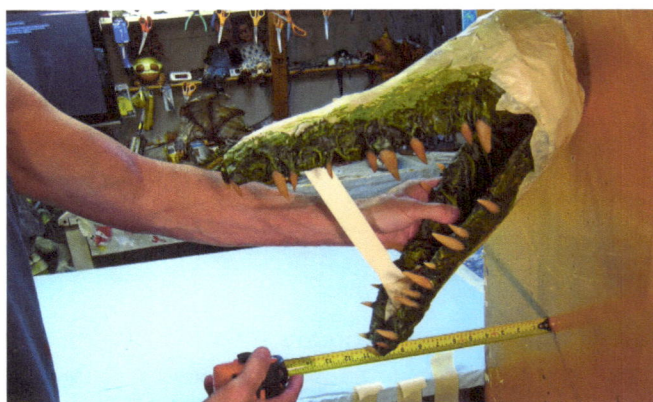

1 For demonstration purposes I'm using a set of jaws that are about 14 inches long. First, assemble the jaws by taping them together in the back. I taped a paint stick inside the jaws to hold them open while I work. Put the jaws against a wall and measure how far the lower jaw sticks out. I use that measurement to replicate the angle off the wall when I put the jaws on my table where it's easier to work.

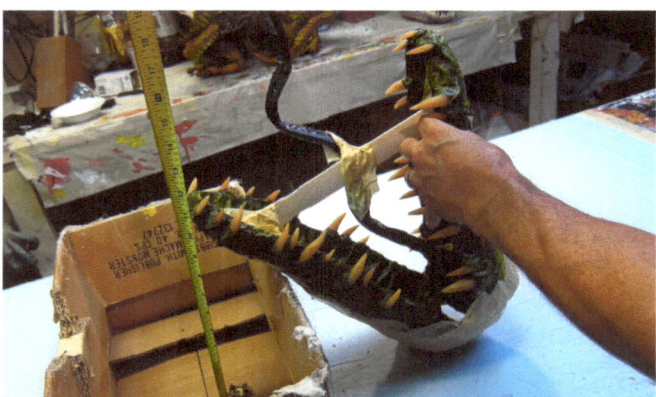
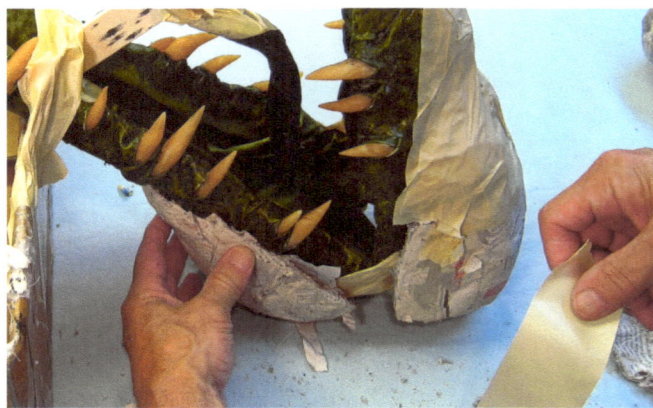

2 Prop the jaws against a box (or something else). Since the lower jaw was 12 inches away from the wall when it was hanging, I made sure it was 12 inches up from the top of the table. Tape the jaws onto the box to hold it in place. Next, tape pieces of mache shell around the base to make it flush with the table.

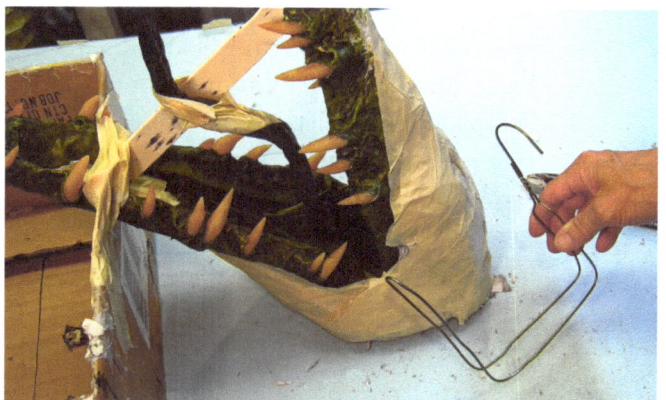 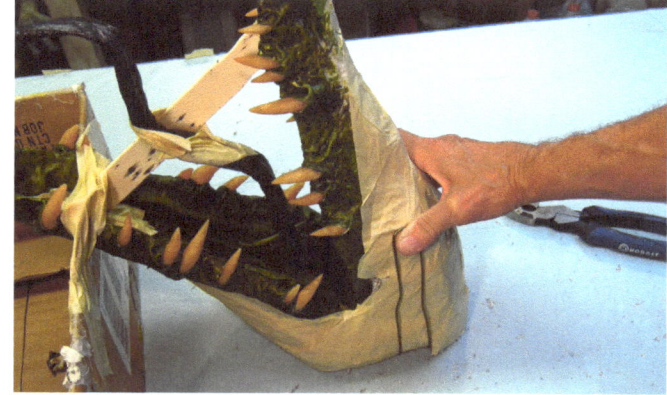

3 As mentioned, I use clothes hangers in my trophies for strength and reinforcement. In this case I stretched a hanger and then bent it into a "U" shape (as wide as the base of the trophy). Then I wrapped the hanger around the base and taped the sides of the U onto the sides of the trophy.

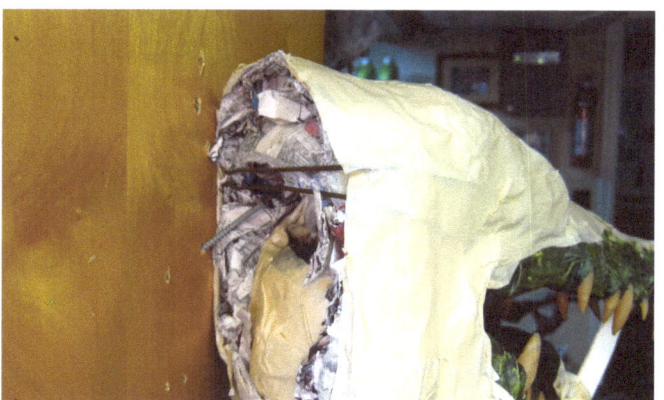 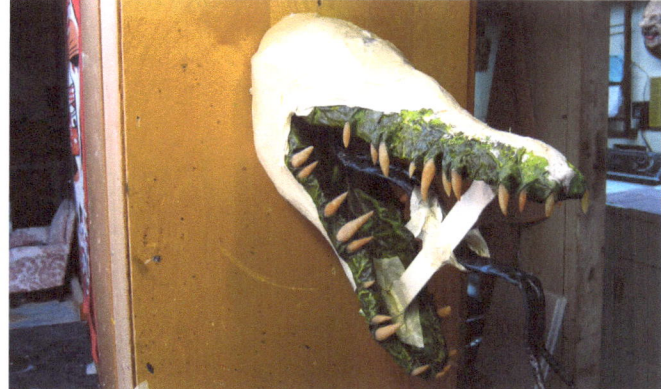

4 This hanger in the back will provide the "hook" for the screw in the wall. This is all the engineering needed for a trophy this size. If the jaws were a lot longer I would run a couple more hangers down the sides of the trophy and connect them in the back for additional strength.

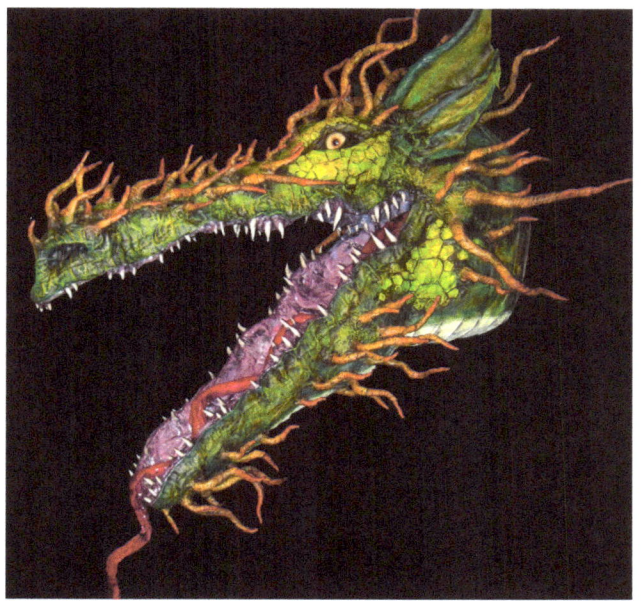

You might have noticed that I added the tongue while the jaws were on the table. I just hot glued the back of the tongue to the back of the jaws. Then I taped it to the stick in the mouth to hold it in place. Once you've successfully hung the jaws on the wall, you can begin sculpting your masterpiece. Sometimes it's easier to work with it on the wall. Other times it's easier to work with it on the table. Sculpt the face of the trophy just like you sculpted the face of the dragon earlier in the book (except you make everything bigger). The photo on the left is just an example of what you can do with a few tentacles and scales. Embellish to your heart's delight.

I'll leave this trophy at this stage and show you how to engineer trophies on plaques.

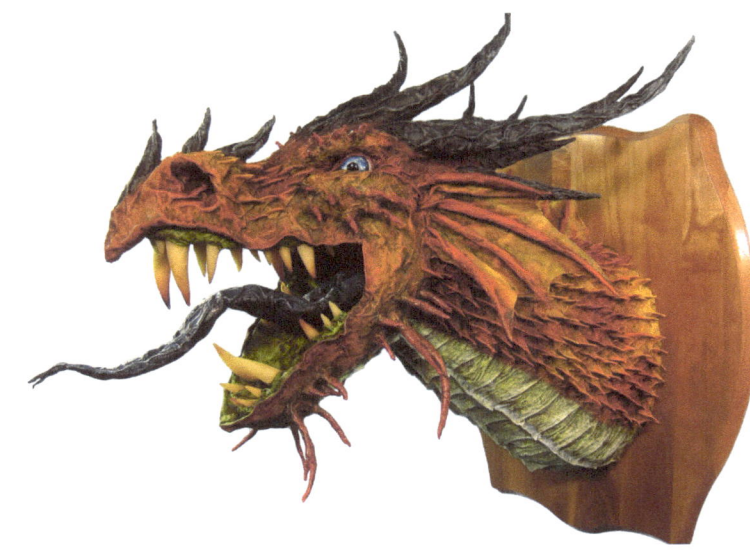

While you don't need a plaque to make a trophy, I think mounting your dragon head on a wooden plaque adds a nice touch. It gives a professional dragon-slayer look to your project. You can buy wooden plaques from any taxidermy company. They come in many sizes and shapes and types of wood.

I'll show you how to make the trophy on the left. But these instructions should work with many trophy variations. For additional clarity watch the time-lapse video of this trophy being made. (See "From the Author" in the back.)

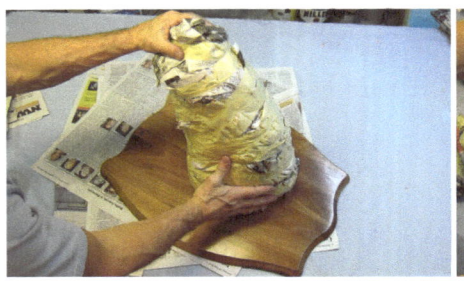

1 Fashion a neck by crumpling several wads of paper and taping them together.

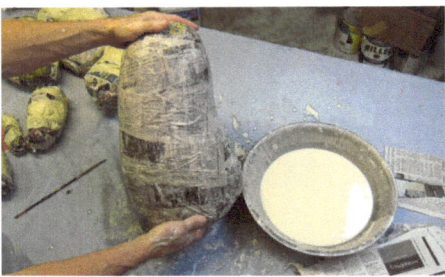

2 Add the paper mache. Make this a little thicker than usual, 7 or 8 layers of paper.

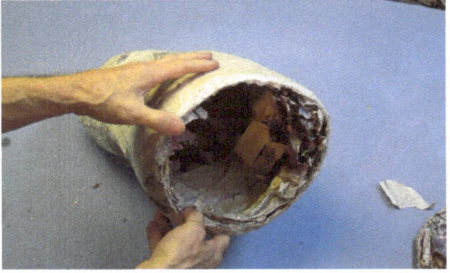

3 After the neck is dry cut off the bottom and pull out the wads of paper. This makes the trophy much lighter.

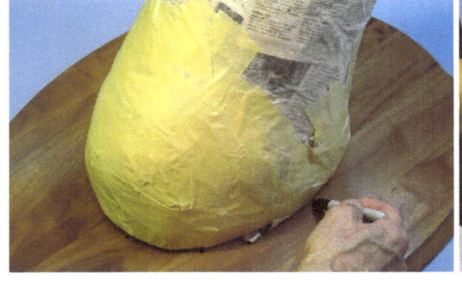

4 Use pieces of paper mache shell (along with masking tape) to make the back of the neck flush against the plaque. Use a Sharpie to mark six dots on the plaque. Make them equidistant (roughly) around the neck.

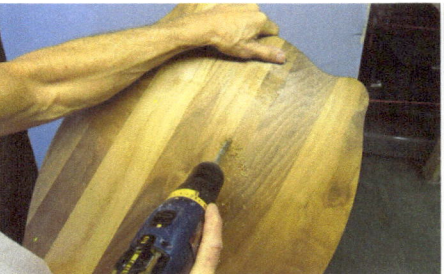

5 You need to drill some holes after that. First turn over the plaque and drill a hole that will fit over the mounting screw in the wall. Drill at the same angle (again roughly) as the screw in the wall. Put the hole about ⅓ of the way down the plaque in the middle. I used a ⅜ inch drill bit for this hole.

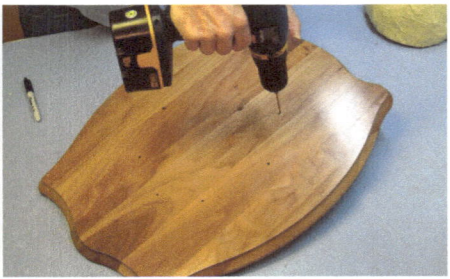

6 Then drill smaller, ⅛ inch, holes through the six dots made with the Sharpie. You drill those from the front.

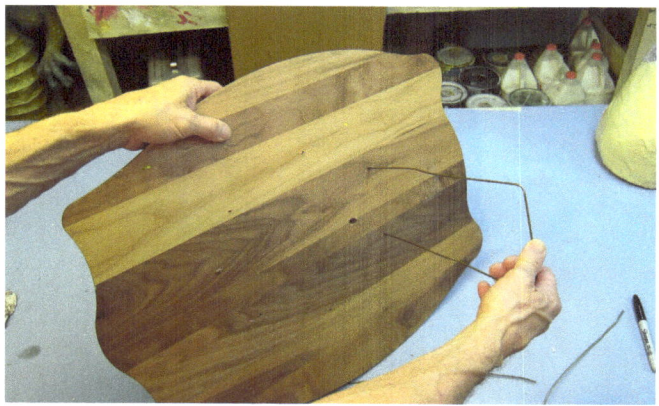
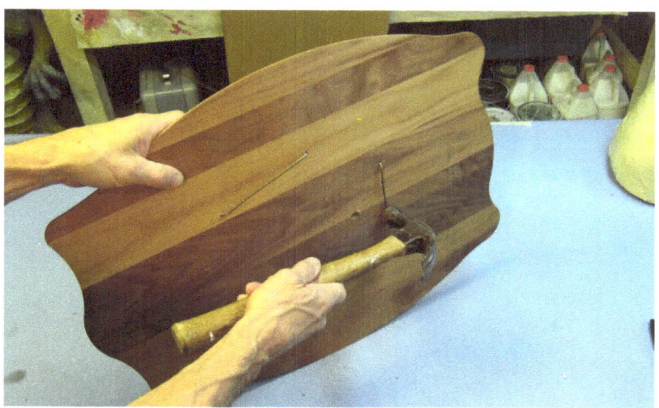

7 Straighten three clothes hangers. Bend each into a "U" shape. Make the bottom of the U the same length as the distance between any two of the holes. Push each of these hangers through the holes in the back of the plaque.

8 Sometimes the U doesn't fit perfectly into the two holes. If this happens, use a hammer to pound on the wires until they are tight against the wood.

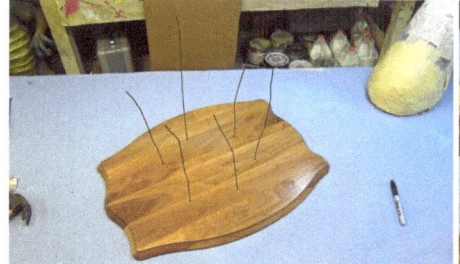
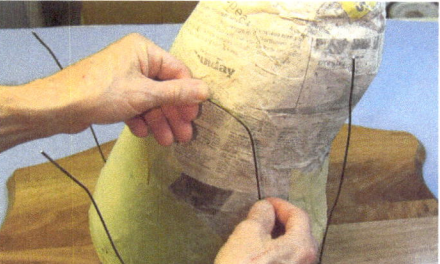
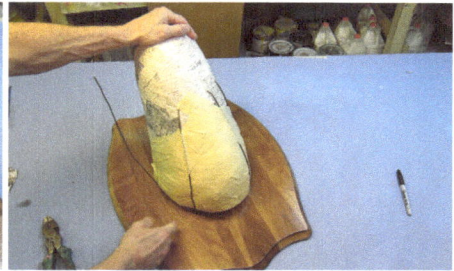

9 Now there will be six wires sticking through the plaque. Bend the ends of each and punch them into the neck. These bends in the wire are important because they "grab" the neck. The wires are smooth. Without the bends the weight of the neck and head can cause the wire to slip (to move under the tape) allowing the trophy to separate from the plaque.

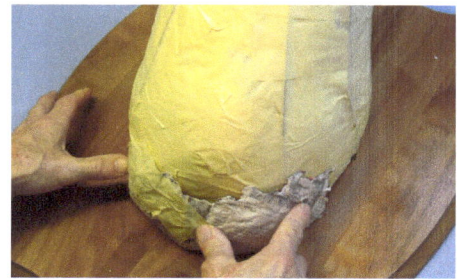
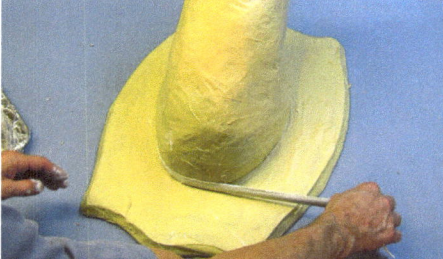
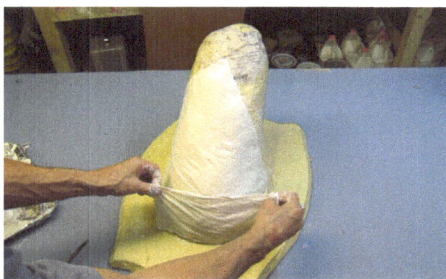

10 After taping down all the wires, once again fill any gaps between the neck and the plaque with pieces of paper mache shell.

11 Put masking tape over the plaque to protect the wood. Before adding the head, it's good to strengthen the neck further by adding cloth mache. Begin by folding a long strip of cloth and wrapping it around the base of the neck.

12 Then add some bigger pieces of cloth around the rest of the neck. This work on the plaque and the neck will provide a really strong armature for the trophy. Not that this could take a few days to dry thoroughly. I know...patience isn't easy.

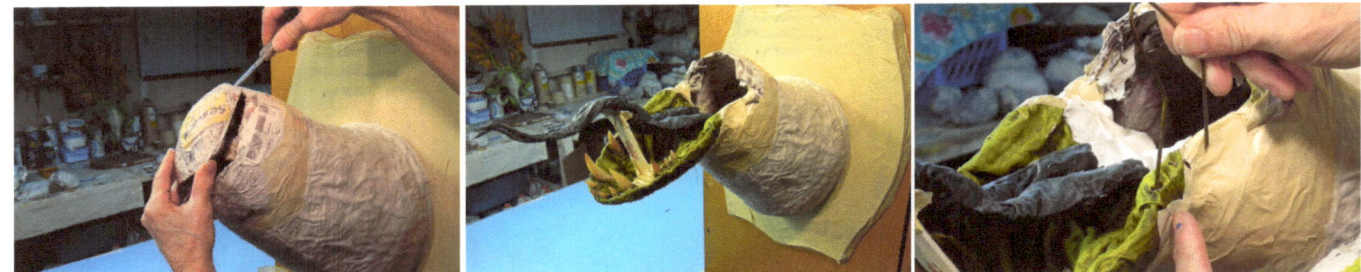

13 Now the fun begins. You get to start building the head. I hung the trophy on the wall for this step. Cut off the end of the neck. Insert the lower jaw into the hole and tape it into place. Add the tongue. Hot glue it into the back of the lower jaw. I reinforced that area by adding a couple pieces of cloth dipped in glue to the back of the mouth. I also used a piece of paint stick to hold the tongue up while the cloth dried. I knew that it was going to be a little tricky keeping this particular upper jaw in place. So I used two small pieces of clothes hanger, one for each side of the jaw, to help out. I bent them into "V-like" shapes (see the photo above on the right). I punched the two ends of the V into the lower jaw.

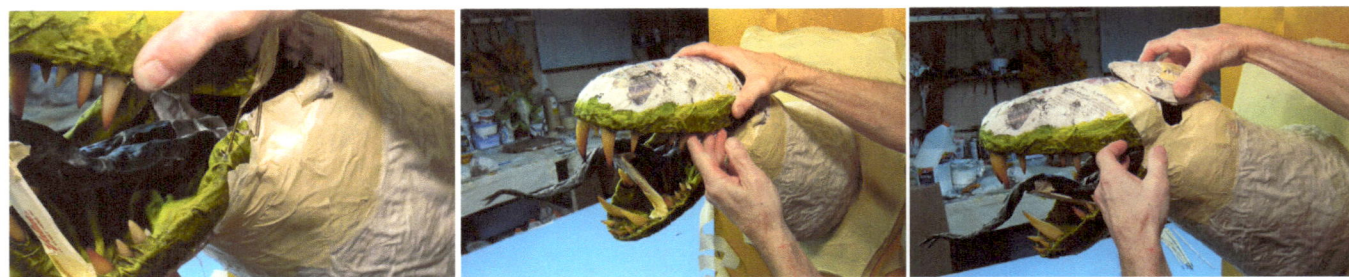

14 I cut small holes in the upper jaw right above those pieces of hanger and pushed it onto the point of the Vs. Then I added masking tape to hold it in place. I used the shell of another mache ball to fill in the gap between the upper jaw and the neck. Note: The wire supports are not absolutely necessary. The shell I added, along with all of the sculpting that occurs later, would hold the upper jaw in place. Alternately I could have put a stick inside the mouth to hold the jaws open while I finished sculpting (like I did with the simple trophy earlier). The truth is that there are several ways to attach the top of the head. Use wire, extra mache shell, and masking tape to attach the top jaw of your trophy.

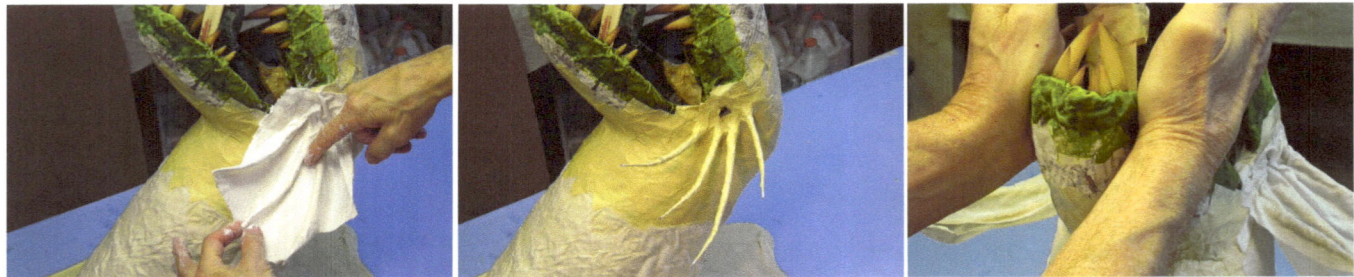

15 I added some ears like the ones I made earlier. You can tell that I really like this kind wing-like ear. From here on it's just a matter of adding embellishments that you like. Be bold. Change what you don't like. For example, it occurred to me that the lower jaw was too wide. So I squished it together (middle photo). I'm not going to go into great detail for the last steps of this build. Most of what I will show you next has already been explained. So I'll briefly show you what I did to finish this trophy. But I'm going to challenge you, for the last time, to experiment with horns and whiskers or tentacles. Use wads of paper to sculpt cheeks or jowls or brows. Keep playing until you hear yourself exclaim, "It's perfect!"

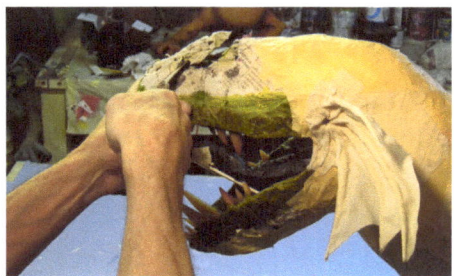 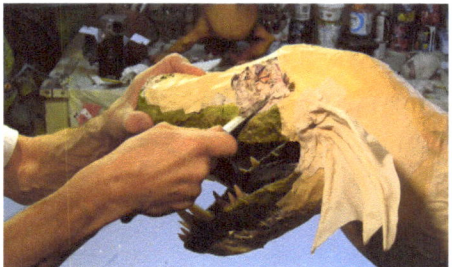 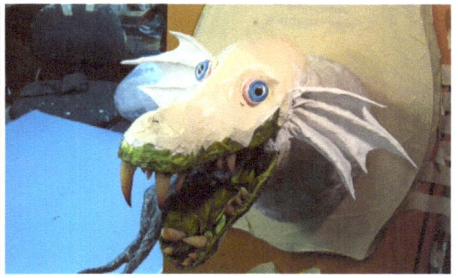

16 The top of the head seemed too round. So I hacked off some of the mache shell with my knife (making sure not to cut the cloth inside the jaws) and added some tape. Then I cut indentations for the eyes which I hot glued in place. For this trophy I used the glass eye "blanks" I mentioned earlier. I painted my own bright blue irises (something that doesn't often occur in nature).

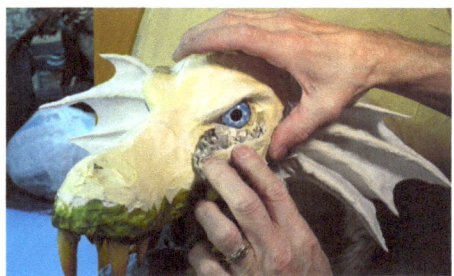 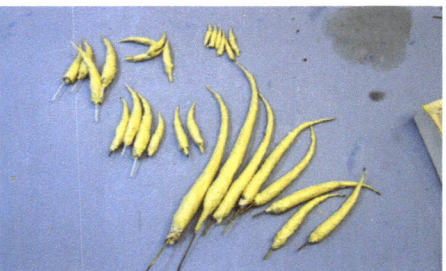 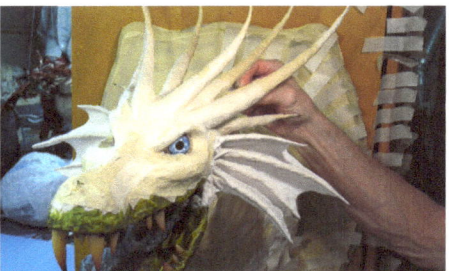

17 Using crumpled paper and masking tape, I made brows and cheeks. I wanted lots of horns on this trophy....well, I always want lots of horns on my trophies. I made those just like I made the "fingers" of the Wyvern. I just made them shorter and thicker. True to my message, I didn't have a plan for the horns. I just put them on, took some off, and put more on until I found what I thought looked good.

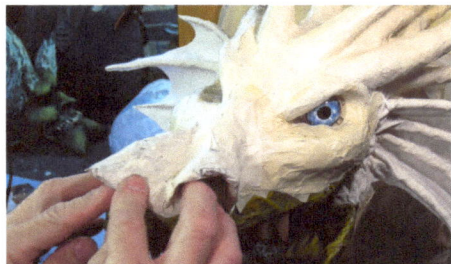 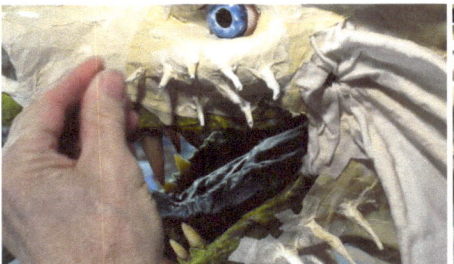 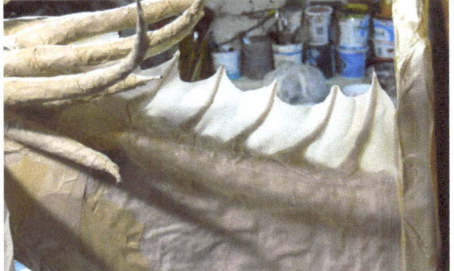

18 I used the shell of two small balls to construct a nose. I also added a few little whiskers. I put some spines down the back that I draped with cloth and trimmed.

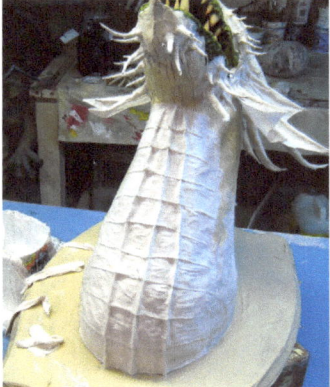 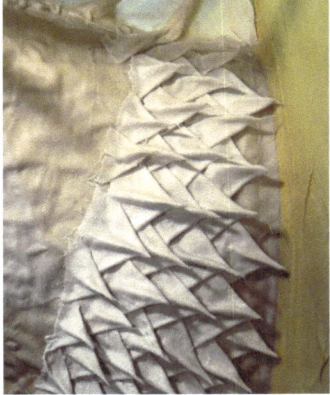

19 I added breast plates and scales the way I usually do. However, this time I pinched each scale in the middle. That is called a "keeled" scale on a reptile. I should mention that you don't need to add scales to make a great trophy. A good paint job will suffice. But it is nice to break up big spaces. I've shown you a couple of different scales in this book. There are other variations. You can see them in the photos of some of my other dragons.

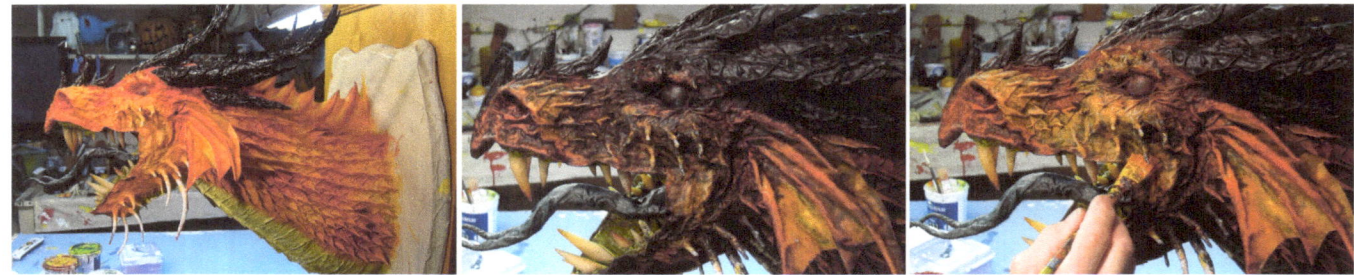

20 I gave this dragon a kind of blotchy paint job using yellow and red. Of course I "ruined" it with blackwash, but then miraculously fixed it with a few highlights.

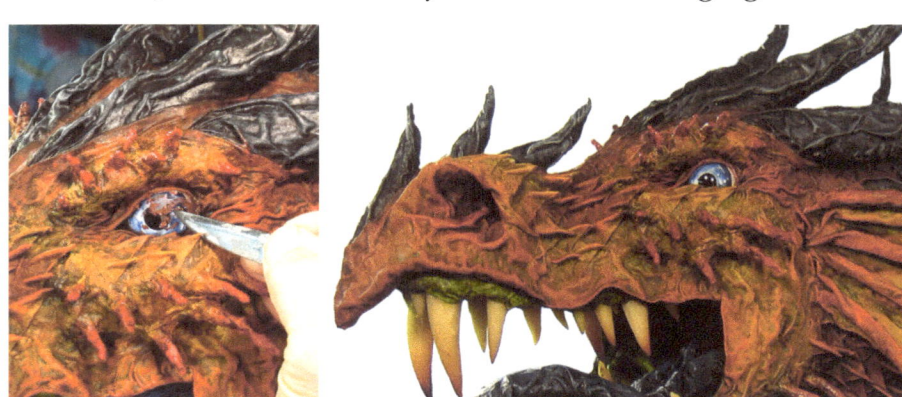

21 As always, with my heart pumping, I scraped the paint off the glass eyes. Another dragon came to life! Makes me (almost) want to cry every time.

If you just finished your first paper mache project, then I'm going to tell you what I always tell new paper mache artists. Your first project is about learning techniques. While I'm sure you love this first project, your second will be your masterpiece. I know there were parts of this build that were challenging. But you got through them and learned from them. You'll be amazed how much easier things get the second time around. So take a break, then make something else. Keep making art. It makes the world a better place.

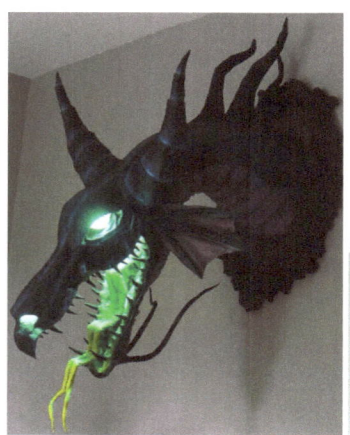

"Maleficent"

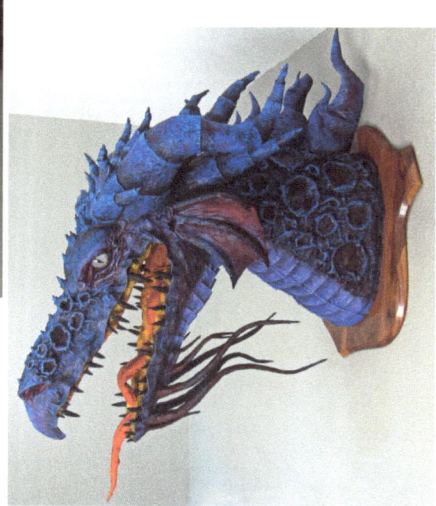

"Son of Maleficent"

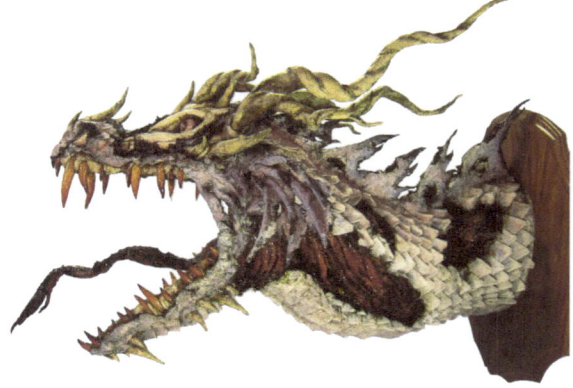

"Zombie Dragon"

From the Author

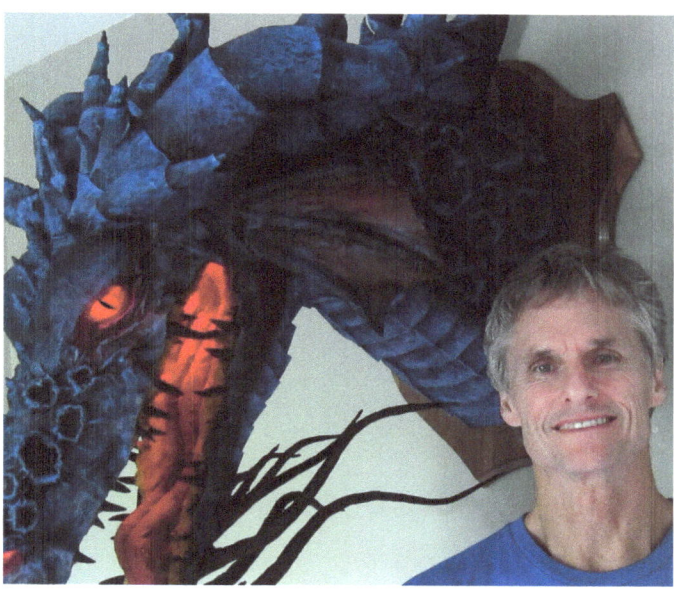

I live in Seattle, Washington. I've been doing paper mache since 1972 when I first made monsters along with my fifth grade students. Those kids loved that project, and so did I. After all of these years I still love working in this medium. It feeds me the right way. Pulling dragons and other creatures out of the ether is supremely satisfying. Maybe it all goes back to those early years of making "Screamers" and seeing the joy and pride on those kids' faces, but it has always seemed important to me to share this creative outlet with other people. It's just too good to keep to myself. Every time I get a photo or a note from some happy person who has used my methods to make a dragon or a monster, I get a vicarious thrill. It makes me feel like a grandparent. It gives me great pleasure to share their creative exuberance. Which is why I'd love to see photos of your dragon. Better yet, let me post a photo on my site. I really enjoy showing off other people's art.

I have published a bunch of books over the years. I have one other still in print besides this one. It is <u>Papier Mâché Monsters: Turning Trinkets and Trash into Magnificent Monstrosities</u> (2009, Gibbs Smith Publisher). The main tutorial in that book involves making a monster, still a great activity for beginners. I wrote my <u>Dragon-maker's Handbook</u> because of the intense, special interest surrounding my dragons. This is the updated version of that handbook. I hope you enjoyed it.

Find more information about me and my art at GourmetPaperMache.com. While you are there check out the photos I mentioned that people have sent to me. Visit my blog, PaperMacheBlog.com, to see what I'm currently working on, and don't forget to subscribe to my YouTube channel (Gourmet Paper Mache) to get alerts when I post new videos. There you can find all of my time-lapse videos along with a couple of other surprises. Note that you won't find any advertisements on my videos. None. Ever.

Questions? You can reach me at dan@gourmetpapermache.com.

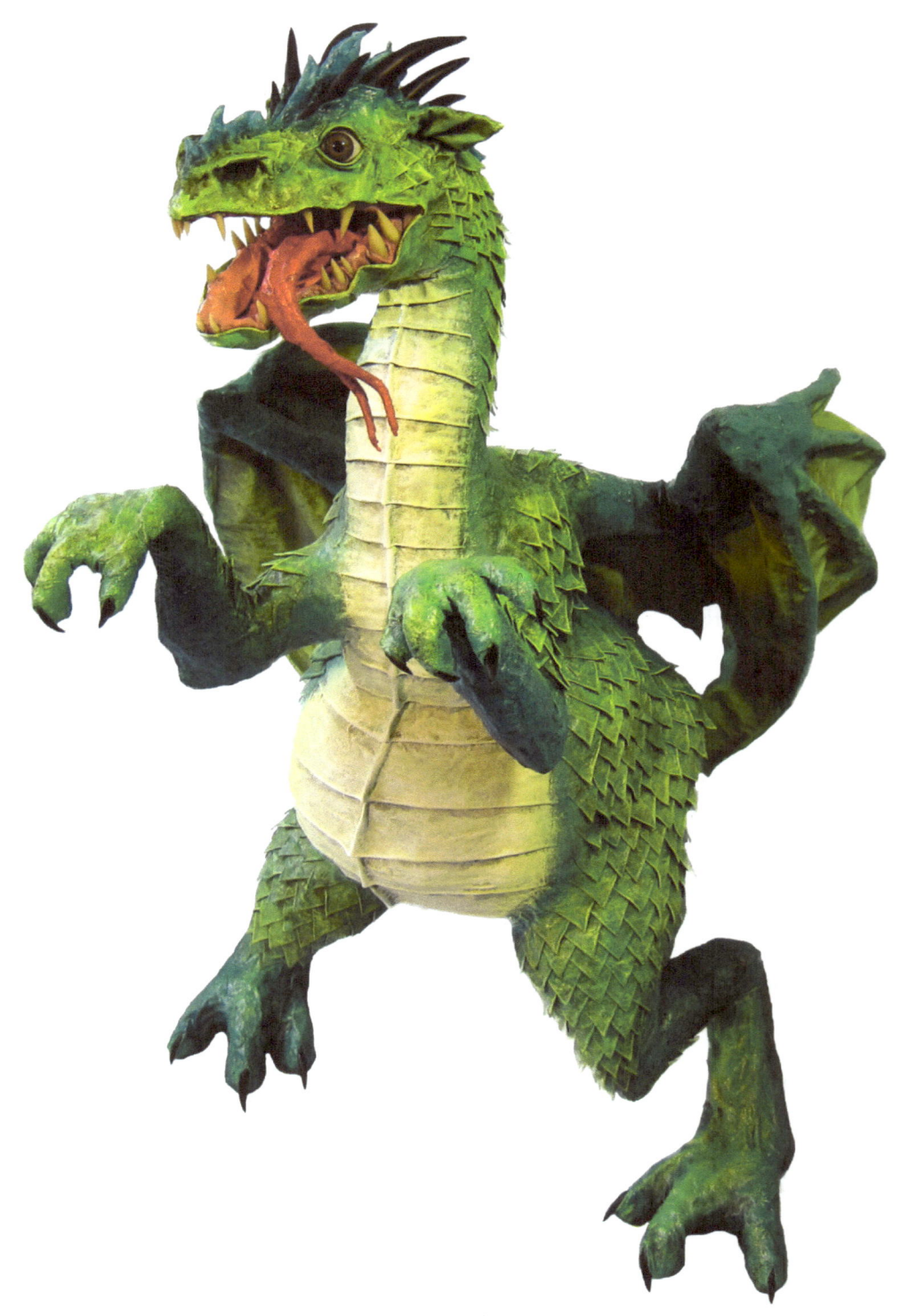

"Dragon Toddler"

www.ingramcontent.com/pod-product-compliance
Lightning Source LLC
Chambersburg PA
CBHW050824180526
45159CB00004B/1781